Children of the Sun

By Hilary Fannin,
after Gorky

T0314580

methuen | drama
LONDON • NEW YORK • OXFORD • NEW DELHI • SYDNEY

METHUEN DRAMA
Bloomsbury Publishing Plc
50 Bedford Square, London, WC1B 3DP, UK
1385 Broadway, New York, NY 10018, USA
29 Earlsfort Terrace, Dublin 2, Ireland

BLOOMSBURY, METHUEN DRAMA and the Methuen
Drama logo are trademarks of Bloomsbury Publishing Plc

First published in Great Britain 2024

Cover design: Rebecca Heselton

Cover image © Ros Kavanagh and AAD

A catalogue record for this book is available from the British Library.

A catalog record for this book is available from the Library of Congress.

ISBN: PB: 978-1-3505-1107-1
ePDF: 978-1-3505-1108-8
eBook: 978-1-3505-1109-5

Series: Modern Plays

Typeset by Mark Heslington Ltd, Scarborough, North Yorkshire
Printed and bound in Great Britain

To find out more about our authors and books visit
www.bloomsbury.com and sign up for our newsletters.

Rough Magic and the Abbey Theatre present

Children of the Sun

By Hilary Fannin, after Gorky

Children of the Sun

By Hilary Fannin, after Gorky

Children of the Sun was commissioned by Rough Magic as part of its COMPASS programme and received its world premiere in a co-production between Rough Magic and the Abbey Theatre at the Abbey Theatre, Dublin on 18 April 2024 with the following cast and creative team.

Cast (in alphabetical order)

Melania	Fiona Bell
Troshin	Colin Campbell
Vagin	John Cronin
Chepurnoy	Brian Doherty
Misha	Rowan Finken
Lusha	Eavan Gaffney
Protasov	Stuart Graham
Elena	Aislín McGuckin
Roman	Peter Newington
Lisa	Rebecca O'Mara
Yegor	Ian Toner

Director	Lynne Parker
Set Design	Sarah Bacon
Costume Design	Sorcha Ní Fhloinn
Lighting Design	Sarah Jane Shiels
Composition & Sound Design	Mel Mercier
Assistant Director	Lianne O'Shea
Assistant Sound Design	Aoife Kavanagh
Hair & Make Up	Val Sherlock
Voice Director	Andrea Ainsworth
Casting Director	Deborah Pearce

Literary Translation by Olga Taranova

For Rough Magic

Producer	Sara Cregan
General Manager	Gemma Reeves
Literary Manager	Karin McCully
Communications & Development Officer	Liza Cox

For the Abbey Theatre

Producer	Craig Flaherty

Production Manager	Anthony Hanley
Company Manager	Danny Erskine
Producing Assistant	Clara Purcell
Technical Production Coordinator	Justin Murphy
Head of Costume and Costume Hire	Donna Geraghty
Costume Supervisor	Síofra Ní Chiardha
Costume Maker	Tara Mulvihill
Costume Assistant	Yvonne Kelly
Breakdown Artist	Sandra Gibney
Laundry and Maintenance Supervisor	Vicky Miller
Costume Dresser	Iseult Deane
Props Supervisor	Adam O'Connell
Chief LX	Simon Burke
LX Programmer	Jonathan Daley
Sound Supervisor	Morgan Dunne
Sound Engineers	Derek Conaghy, Leon Henry
Marketing	Heather Maher, John Tierney
Publicity	Conleth Teevan
Social Media	Jack O'Dea
Irish Sign Language Interpreter	Ali Stewart
Audio Describer	Bríd Ní Ghruagáin
Captioner	Michael Poynor
Artistic Director/Co-Director	Caitríona McLaughlin
Executive Director/Co-Director	Mark O'Brien

Production Credits

Company Stage Manager	Orla Burke
Deputy Stage Manager	Tara Furlong
Assistant Stage Manager	Emily Rose Champion
Costume Tailor	Gillian Carew
Design Assistants	Maybelle Rainey, Harry Wainright, Ruth Keogh
Set Construction	Connacht Production Services
Publicity Image	Ros Kavanagh
Production Photography	Ros Kavanagh

Children of the Sun was developed in association with the Theatre Royal Waterford.

Hilary Fannin
Writer

Hilary is an award-winning playwright, novelist and newspaper columnist. Born in Dublin, where she still lives, she was writer in association at the Abbey Theatre in its centenary year, 2004. Her plays, including *Mackerel Sky*, *Doldrum Bay*, *Famished Castle* and an adaptation of Racine's *Phaedra*, have been performed in Ireland, London, Europe and North America.

For a decade she wrote a weekly column for *The Irish Times*, having previously been the newspaper's TV critic, and was named Irish Broadsheet Columnist of the Year in 2019. Her memoir, *Hopscotch*, was published to critical acclaim in 2015. Her first novel, *The Weight of Love*, was published in 2020, winning the John McGahern Award for debut Irish fiction. She was the 2021 Writer Fellow at the Oscar Wilde Centre, Trinity College Dublin, and is currently working on her second novel.

Lynne Parker
Director

Lynne is Artistic Director and co-founder of Rough Magic Theatre Company.

Productions for Rough Magic include *Freefalling* by Georgina Miller (with Lime Tree | Belltable, Limerick); *The Tempest* by William Shakespeare (with Kilkenny Arts Festival 2022); *All the Angels* by Nick Drake (with Smock Alley 2021); *Solar Bones* by Mike McCormack in an adaptation by Michael West (Kilkenny Arts Festival 2020, the Abbey Theatre 2022); *Hecuba* by Marina Carr (Dublin Theatre Festival 2019); *Cleft* by Fergal McElherron (glór, GIAF, KAF, 2019); *A Midsummer Night's Dream* (Kilkenny Arts Festival 2018); *Melt* (Dublin Theatre Festival 2017); *The House Keeper* (Best New Play 2012); *Don Carlos* (Best Production 2007); *The Taming of the Shrew* (Best Production 2006); *Improbable Frequency* (Best Production, Best Director 2004); *Copenhagen* (Best Production 2002); *Pentecost* (Best Irish Production, Dublin Theatre Festival 1995) and by Declan Hughes *Digging for Fire* (London Time Out Award 1992); *New Morning*, *Love and a Bottle* and *Shiver*.

Other theatre credits include *You Belong To Me* (Once Off and Smock Alley); *Beowulf* (Tron); *Heavenly Bodies*, *The Sanctuary Lamp*, *Down the Line* (Abbey); *The Drawer Boy* (Galway International Arts Festival); *The Girl Who Forgot to Sing Badly* (Theatre Lovett); *Macbeth* (Lyric); also productions for Charabanc, Druid, the Gate, the Bush, the Almeida, the Old Vic, West Yorkshire Playhouse, Birmingham Rep and Teatrul National Bucharest.

Lynne Parker was awarded the Irish Times Special Tribute Award in 2008 and an Honorary Doctorate from Trinity College Dublin in 2010. Lynne most recently received the 2020 Best Director Award at the Irish Times Irish Theatre Awards for *Solar Bones*.

Fiona Bell
Melania

Theatre credits include *Oedipus*, *The Dead*, *Only an Apple*, *Pygmalion*, *Major Barbara*, *Three Sisters*, *A Month in the Country*, *Medea* (The Abbey Theatre); *Hamlet*, *Tribes*, *Who's Afraid of Virginia Woolf*, *The Father*, *Jane Eyre*, *Wuthering Heights*, *The Vortex*, *The Price*, *A Boston Marriage*, *Present Laughter*, *An Enemy of the People*, *See You Next Tuesday*, *Pride and Prejudice* (The Gate Theatre); *Leaves*, *The Last Return* (Druid Theatre Company); *The Country*, *Further than the Furthest Thing* (Hatch Theatre Company); *Strandline*, *Spinning* (Fishamble Theatre Company); *Dinner With Friends* (Guna Nua); *Henry VI, Parts 1, 2 and 3*), *Richard III* (RSC); *Good*, *Macbeth*, *Mate in Three*, *Brilliant Traces*, *Cinderella* (Tron Theatre, Glasgow); *Mirandolina*, *Bedroom Farce*, *Dancing at Lughnasa*, *Oleanna*, *The Masterbuilder* (Lyceum Theatre, Edinburgh); *Jump the Life to Come*, *The Lament for Arthur Cleary* (7.84); *Snake* (Hampstead); *Animal* (Soho Theatre); *Sacred Hearts* and *Cyrano de Bergerac* (Communicado, Scotland).

Film and television credits include *The Woman in the Wall* (BBC); *Crime II* (ITVX); *Granite Harbour* (BBC); *Kin* (RTÉ); *The Nest* (Studio Lambert); *Blood II* (Virgin Media); *Dead Still* (RTÉ); *Shetland* (ITV); *Casualty* (BBC); *EastEnders* (BBC); *Manhunters* (BBC); *Low Winter Sun* (Tiger Aspect); *Soldier Soldier* (Granada); *Taggart* (STV); *Silent Roar* (Chris Young Productions); *Finding You* (Sky); *Loving Miss Hatto* (Metropolitan); *Trainspotting* (Channel 4 Films) and *Gregory's 2 Girls* (Channel 4 Films).

Colin Campbell
Troshin

Colin holds a Bachelor in Acting degree from the Lir Academy at Trinity College, Dublin (in partnership with RADA).

Recent stage credits include the role of Tom in Eoghan Quinn's *Colic* directed by Annabelle Comyn for Hatch Theatre Company and Pavilion Theatre; the title role in Livin' Dred's production of *Tarry Flynn* directed by Aaron Monaghan and the role of Karl in Emmet Kirwan's *Straight to Video* directed by Phillip McMahon for Landmark Productions.

Colin toured internationally with the Shakespeare's Globe Touring Ensemble performing in plays *Twelfth Night*, *The Comedy of Errors* and *Pericles*.

Other recent credits include Marina Carr's adaptation of Virginia Woolf's *To the Lighthouse* directed by Annabelle Comyn for Hatch Theatre Company and The Everyman Cork; the role of Barry in *Flights* directed by Thomas Martin at The Project Arts Centre and Clapham Omnibus; *Cuckoo* directed by Debbie Hannan at the Soho Theatre; *Scotties* with Theatre Gu Leor, the National Theatre of Scotland and the Abbey Theatre; the role of Pig opposite Evanna Lynch in the 20th Anniversary production of Enda Walsh's *Disco Pigs* directed by John Haidar at Trafalgar Studios, London, with performances at the Irish Repertory Theatre, New York in 2018; the role of Jimmy in the Corn Exchange production *Dublin by Lamplight*, directed by Annie Ryan for the Abbey Theatre; Manus in Ingmar Bergman's *Through a Glass Darkly*, directed by Annie Ryan for Corn Exchange; *Hostel 16* directed by Raymond Keane and *Council of Nicea* directed by Iseult Golden, at Smock Alley Theatre; the rehearsed reading *All That Is*, directed by Ronan Phelan for Druid Theatre Company and Eccles Theatre Group's *The Windstealers* directed by Anushka Senanayake at Smock Alley Theatre.

John Cronin
Vagin

Theatre credits include *The Tempest*, *Glue, Digging for Fire* (Rough Magic); *It was Easy (In the End)*, *The Comedy of Errors*, *Saved, The Resistible Rise of Arturo Ui, Romeo and Juliet* (Abbey Theatre); *Country Music* (Glass Mask Theatre); *Staging the Treaty, Sunder, On*

Corporation Street, Pals (Anu); *The Treaty*, *The End of the Road* (Fishamble); *Restorations* (Project Arts Centre); *Before Monsters Were Made* (15th Oak); *A View from the Bridge, My Cousin Rachel*, *Glengarry Glen Ross* (Gate Theatre); *Othello* (Second Age); *I am My Own Wife* (Prime Cut); *Richard III* (Fast & Loose); *Observe the Sons of Ulster Marching Towards the Somme* (Livin Dred); *The Anatomy of a Seagull* (Loose Canon); *The Last Days of Judas Iscariot* (Making Strange); *Stuck* (Project Arts Centre) and *Stones in His Pockets* (Duchess Theatre).

Film and television credits include *This Town* (Kudos Films/BBC One); *The Doll Factory* (Paramount+); *The Tourist S2* (BBC One); *Fair City* (RTÉ); *Slice the Thief* (Dublin Port Film); *Rebellion*, *Resistance* (RTÉ); *Black 47* (Fastnet Films); *The Foreigner* (Netflix); *Trial of the Century* (TV3); *Y Sycras* (Fatti Films); *Trivia* (RTÉ); *Jack Taylor* (Telegael); *Insatiable* (Kirby Films); *Legend* (RTÉ); *The General* (Merlin Films); *The Last Bus Home* (Bandit Films); *Family* (BBC) and *The Commitments* (20th Century Fox).

Brian Doherty
Chepurnoy

Theatre credits include *All the Angels, Hecuba, Pentecost* and *Improbable Frequency* (Rough Magic); *Translations*, *The Wake*, *Three Sisters*, *Down the Line* and *Tarry Flynn* (Abbey Theatre); *The Seagull, Sive* and *Famine* (Druid); *Common* and *Aristocrats* (Royal National Theatre); *Antony and Cleopatra*, *The Winter's Tale*, *Little Eagles*, *The Drunks*, *Macbeth, God in Ruins* and *Great Expectations* (RSC); *The Father, From Here to Eternity, Stones in His Pockets* (West End); *Tomcat* (Papatango); *A Steady Rain* (Theatre Royal Bath); *Narratives* (Royal Court); *The Red Iron*, *Happy Birthday Dear Alice, The Crucible* (Red Kettle) and *Evening Train* (The Everyman, Cork).

Film and television credits include *Blackshore, Hidden Assets, The Woman in the Wall, A Thousand Blows, Resistance, Trigonometry, Witless*, *Raw*, *Pure Mule, Fair City*, *Casualty* and *Glenroe*, *Dreamhorse*, *A Street Cat Named Bob*, *Perrier's Bounty* and *Garage*.

Rowan Finken
Misha

Rowan is originally from west Cork and is a graduate of the Lir, National Academy of Dramatic Art in association with RADA and Trinity College Dublin.

He most recently appeared on stage in *The Making of Mollie*, directed by Sarah Baxter at the Ark and *Eastland*, directed by Anne Bogart, produced by The Collective at the Samuel Beckett Theatre. Other recent theatre credits include Rough Magic's *The Tempest*, as part of the Kilkenny Arts Festival in the role of Ferdinand and *Staging The Treaty*, for Anú.

Eavan Gaffney
Lusha

Since graduating from the Lir Academy in 2020 Eavan's credits include *You're Still Here* by Murmuration for the Dublin Fringe Festival, *The Fabulously True and Timeless Tale of Sergeant Virgil* by Andy Crook for Faoin Speir (Longford Arts Office) and theatre works-in-progress and rehearsed readings with Caitriona Daly, Annie Keegan, Annabelle Comyn, Aoife Spillane-Hinks and Nessa Matthews.

Eavan most recently performed in Emilie Hetland's *Revolutionary,* directed by Katie O'Halloran, and in *Staging the Treaty* written by Theo Dorgan and directed by Louise Lowe. Just prior she played the role of Maud alongside Owen Roe in Sebastian Barry's *The Steward of Christendom* at the Gate Theatre, Dublin.

In 2021 Eavan performed for President Higgins at Áras an Úachtaráin for Bloomsday 2021, and was selected to participate in *Conversations on a Playwright*, a week of masterclasses on the plays of Tom Murphy. Eavan features in the Abbey Theatre's *Unseen Plays* radio play series as Sadie in *The Wood of the Whispering* directed by Maisie Lee, and has worked on screen projects with Louise Lowe (*Canaries,* 2020) and Kate Dolan (*Pillow Queens: Holy Show*).

Stuart Graham
Protasov

Theatre credits include *Northern Star*, *New Morning* (Rough Magic); *The Ferryman* (Royal Court/West End/Broadway); *The Force of*

Change (Royal Court); *Molly Sweeney* (Print Room); *Observe the Sons of Ulster Marching Towards the Somme*, *The Well of the Saints* (Abbey Theatre); *In a Little World of Our Own*, *As the Beast Sleeps*, *A Number* (Peacock Theatre); *Da* (Gate Theatre); *Macbeth*, *Hamlet*, *Carthaginians*, *Rough Beginnings*, *The Tempest* (Lyric Theatre); *Kelly* and *Du* (Olympia Theatre); *Medea* (Samuel Beckett); *Blackbird* (Decadent Theatre); *Brothers of the Brush* (Arts Theatre) and *The Silver Tassie* (Almeida Theatre).

Film and television credits include *Aisha*, *Hunger*, *Tinker Tailor Soldier Spy*, *The Cured*, *The Informant*, *Bad Day for the Cut*, *The Whistleblower*, *Song for a Raggy Boy*, *Michael Collins*, *The Butcher Boy*, *Awaydays*, *Goldfish Memory*, *The Bargain Shop*, *Small Engine Repair*, *Volkswagen Joe*, *The Great Train Robbery*, *The Window*, *One Man's Hero*, *Parked*, *Milo*, *Shadow Dancer*, *Misery Harbour*, *Mary Shelley*, *The Foreigner*, *The Sins*, *Silent Witness*, *Vera*, *Smother*, *North Sea Connection*, *The Clinic*, *The Interrogation of Tony Martin*, *The Secret*, *Dalgliesh*, *Professionals*, *Harry Wild*, *The Fall*, *Thirteen*, *The Frankenstein Chronicles*, *Egypt*, *The Last Post*, *As the Beast Sleeps* and *The Wheel of Time*.

Aislín McGuckin
Elena

Aislín McGuckin's theatre credits include *Hecuba* and *Famished Castle* (Rough Magic); *Tartuffe*, *Come on Home* and *Heartbreak House* (Abbey Theatre); *Audrey or Sorrow* (Landmark Productions and Abbey Theatre); *Richard III* and *Our Father* (Almeida); *The Steward of Christendom* (Royal Court and Gate Theatre); *A Month in the Country* (Gate Theatre); *King Lear* (Theatre Royal Bath); *Macbeth*, *The Homecoming*, *Twelfth Night*, *Henry VI Parts 1, 2 and 3* (RSC); *The Duchess of Malfi* and *Volpone* (Greenwich Theatre); *Dial M for Murder* (West Yorkshire Playhouse); *The Homeplace* and *Dancing at Lughnasa* (Lyric Theatre) and *The Clearing* (Shared Experience).

Film and television credits include *Flora and Son*, *Joyride*, *Normal People* (Element Pictures); *Cold Courage* (Luminoir); *Overshadowed* (Rollem Productions); *The Miniaturist*, *Paula*, *New Tricks*, *Holby City*, *David Copperfield*, *Amongst Women*, *The Creatives* and *Casualty* (BBC); *Oasis* and *Outlander* (Left Bank); *The Unknown Soldier* (Carlton); *The Nephew* (Foxgrange); *Trojan Eddie* (Cairndawn); *The Other Lamb* (Rumble Films); *The Music Room* (Grey Cat) and *The White Countess* (Merchant Ivory).

Peter Newington
Roman

Peter last appeared on stage in *Echo* at Smock Alley Theatre.
Previous theatre credits include *Cuckoo* at London's Soho Theatre
and *Lobsters* at the Project Arts Centre.

Film and television credits include *Calm with Horses*, *Never Grow Old*,
The Rhythm Section, *Blackshore*, *Hope Street* and *The Doll Factory*.
He appeared as the lead in the IFTA nominated short film *Flicker*.

Peter began acting when he joined Dublin Youth Theatre in 2013. He
was cast as Melchior in their production of *Spring Awakening*, which
played at Axis Ballymun as part of the 2014 Dublin Theatre Festival,
and *Show Me Love*, which played at Smock Alley in 2015.

While in UCD, Peter played *Hamlet*, Stanley Stubbers in Richard
Bean's *One Man, Two Guvnors*, Cornwall in *King Lear*, and performed
in *Brief Interviews with Hideous Men*, a stage adaptation of David
Foster Wallace's short stories.

Rebecca O'Mara
Lisa

Theatre credits include *All the Angels*, *Melt* (Rough Magic); *The Quare
Fellow, Othello*, *Aristocrats* (Abbey Theatre); *The Last Return,
Furniture, Helen and I* (Druid); *Describe the Night* (Hampstead
Theatre); *Private Lives*, *Wuthering Heights*, *The Vortex*, *Pride and
Prejudice*, *Mrs Warren's Profession*, *Hayfever*, *The Yalta Game* (Gate
Theatre); *Chekhov's First Play* (Dead Centre); *Moment* (Bush Theatre);
Danton's Death (National Theatre); *Far from the Madding Crowd*
(English Touring Theatre); *Deep Blue Sea* (Theatre Royal Bath/West
End); *Minsk* (Bush Theatre); *Salt Meets Wound* (Theatre503) and
06/07/05 (Arcola).

Film and television credits include *Beetlejuice 2, Anniversary, Smother*,
The Toxic Avenger, *Herself*, *Bump*, *Red Rock*, *Line of Duty*, *Jimmy's
Hall*, *Doctors*, *The History of Mister Polly*.

Awards include the Irish Times Irish Theatre Awards, Best Supporting
Actress (*Furniture* by Sonya Kelly).

Rebecca is the voice of Caitlin in *Thomas and Friends* and trained at
the London Academy of Music and Dramatic Art.

Ian Toner
Yegor

Theatre credits include *The Treaty* (Fishamble); *Punk Rock* (2015 Nominated Best Supporting Actor Irish Times Theatre Award) and *Double Cross* (Lyric Theatre); *Look Back in Anger*, *Romeo and Juliet*, *The Vortex* (Gate Theatre); *These Stupid Things* (Smock Alley); *The Shitstorm* (Peacock Theatre); *Wild Sky* (Bewley's Cafe Theatre, national/international tour); *At the Ford* (The New Theatre/DTF); *Staging the Treaty* (Anu Productions); *The Making of Mollie* (The Ark Theatre).

Film and TV credits include *The Englishman's Papers*, *The Clean-Up Crew* (Hail Mary Productions); *Valhalla* (Netflix); *Titans* (History Channel); *Catch 22* (Paramount/Hulu); *Woman in White* (BBC); *Younger* (TV Land); *Redwater* (BBC); *Cold Case Collins, Rebellion*, *Smother* and *Deadstill* (RTÉ); *An Klondike* (TG4); *We Have Always Lived in the Castle* (Castleblackwood); *The Cured* (Tilted Pictures).

Sarah Bacon
Set Designer

Sarah Bacon trained at the Motley Theatre Design Course in London, having previously studied Architecture and 3D Design in Dublin and Brighton. She is Dublin based and designs for theatre, opera and dance. In 2010 she was a Linbury Prize Finalist and has exhibited her work at the National Theatre in London.

Theatre credits include *The Loved Ones*, *Hecuba*, *Melt*, *The Effect* and *Everything Between Us* (Rough Magic); *The Weir*, *Drama at Inish*, *City Song*, *Anna Karenina*, *The Shadow of a Gunman*, *Luck Just Kissed You Hello* (Abbey Theatre); *The Children*, *Beginning*, *Assassins* and *Look Back in Anger* (Gate Theatre); *Werther*, *Escape from the Seraglio* (INO); *Conversations After Sex* (Thisispopbaby); *The Water Orchard* (Collapsing Horse); and *What Did I Miss?* (The Ark).

Production Design credits include *20 Shots of Opera* (Irish National Opera) and *Dubliners* (Corn Exchange/Smock Alley).

Costume Design credits include *The Cold Sings* (Junk Ensemble); *The Patient Gloria* (Peacock, St Ann's Warehouse) and *The Rehearsal: Playing the Dane* (PanPan).

Sorcha Ní Fhloinn
Costume Designer

Sorcha has worked extensively as a costume designer, maker and supervisor across theatre, film and music videos in Ireland and the UK. She is a graduate of the Postgraduate Diploma in Theatre Costume course at the Royal Academy of Dramatic Art.

Previous design credits include *The Tempest* and *All the Angels* (Rough Magic); *Love + Information* (TUD Grangegorman); *Queenish* by Soulé (Diffusion Lab); *Close Quarters* (RADA Gielgud Theatre); *Test Dummy* (Theatre Upstairs); *Gays Against the Free State!* (Smock Alley Theatre) and *Hornet's Nest* (ANU Productions).

Sarah Jane Shiels
Lighting Designer

SJ began designing lighting in Dublin Youth Theatre, completing an MSc in Interactive Digital Media 2021 and a BA in Drama and Theatre Studies 2006 (Trinity), and the Rough Magic Seeds programme 2006–8. From 2010 to 2017, she was co-artistic director of WillFredd Theatre.

Theatre credits include *Hecuba*, *The Tempest*, *All the Angels*, *Glue*, *Much Ado About Nothing* and *A Portrait of the Artist as a Young Man* (Rough Magic); *One Good Turn*, *This Beautiful Village*, *Jimmy's Hall*, *The Remains of Maise Duggan*, *Town is Dead*, *The Shadow of a Gunman* (Abbey Theatre); *Bellow* (Brokentalkers); *Little Women* (Lyric Theatre); *Peter Pan* (The Gate Theatre); *Hansel and Gretel* (Theatre Lovett and Irish National Opera); *The Tin Soldier*, *FRNKSTN* (Theatre Lovett); *Werther*, *Faust* (Irish National Opera) and *You Belong to Me* (Once Off and Smock Alley).

Mel Mercier
Composer & Sound Designer

Mel Mercier is a freelance, multi-disciplinary, Tony-Award nominated artist with an international reputation as a performer, composer and sound designer. He is Artistic Director of the Irish Gamelan Orchestra, MÓNCKK new music ensemble and PULSUS, the first Irish traditional percussion ensemble. Mel was Professor and Chair of Performing Arts at the University of Limerick from 2016 to 2022.

Introduced to music by his father, Peadar Mercier, Mel collaborated with composer Mícheál Ó Súilleabháin for forty years, and throughout the 1980s he performed internationally with John Cage and Merce Cunningham Dance Company. Mel has created music for theatre in Ireland and internationally for twenty-five years, working regularly with Deborah Warner, Fiona Shaw, Corcadorca and Gare St Lazare Ireland.

Recent creative projects include *The Quare Fellow* (Abbey Theatre, 2023–4); *The Tempest* (dir. Deborah Warner, Ustinov Theatre, Bath, 2022); *Guests of the Nation* (co-devised with Pat Kiernan and Kevin Barry, Cork, 2022 (Corcadorca)); *How It Is* (with Irish Gamelan Orchestra/MÓNCKK/Gare St Lazare Ireland, Cork/London/Dublin 2018–22); *Portia* (Coughlan, Abbey Theatre, 2022).

Awards include Irish Times Theatre Award for Gare St Lazare Ireland's *How It Is – Part I* (2018); Irish Times Theatre Award for Corcadorca's *Far Away* (2017); New York Drama Desk Award and Tony Award nomination for Colm Tóibín's *Testament of Mary* (Broadway 2012).

Rough Magic

Rough Magic is a national, independent theatre company, delivering a comprehensive programme of new Irish writing, reimagined classics, and contemporary international plays, to audiences across Ireland and beyond. Our work is expansive, playful and whatever its form, focused on the moment. Rough Magic provides an unexpected angle to the mainstream and an anchor to the emerging generation.

Over four decades, Rough Magic has established itself as a creative entity and a valued institution; operating as an ensemble across the spectrum of scale and style, offering fresh perspectives and engaging audiences with the qualities that define us – wit, subversion, intellectual rigour, and free artistic expression. Since its foundation in 1984, Rough Magic has produced 140 shows, including forty-four World premieres and twenty-six Irish premieres.

The company is an industry pioneer in artist development, notably through our SEEDS programme for emerging artists, through which many leading theatre makers were introduced to the industry. We believe in showcasing and platforming theatre practitioners at all stages, supporting them to take artistic risks.

In 2021 the company launched COMPASS, folding play development and support for theatre artists into the company's core programme. Under COMPASS we have established partnerships with leading theatres in Limerick, Waterford and Cork to produce a series of major new commissions. *The Loved Ones* by Erica Murray was the first of these commissions to come to the stage, in a co-production with the Gate Theatre, Dublin, supported by our partners at LimeTree I Belltable, Limerick as part of Dublin Theatre Festival 2023.

Awards include: a record number of four Irish Times Theatre Awards for Best Production (*Copenhagen*, *Improbable Frequency*, *The Taming of the Shrew*, *Don Carlos*); London Time Out Award; two Edinburgh Fringe First Awards and the Irish Times Theatre Award for Best Ensemble for *A Midsummer Night's Dream*. Most recently Rough Magic's production of *Solar Bones* won Best Actor for Stanley Townsend and Best Director for Lynne Parker at the Irish Times Theatre Awards.

Rough Magic's COMPASS programme is supported by the Lackendarragh Bursary. Rough Magic is proudly supported by the Arts Council.

Abbey Theatre

As Ireland's National Theatre, the Abbey Theatre's ambition is to enrich the cultural lives of everyone with a curiosity for and interest in Irish theatre, stories, artists and culture. Courage and imagination are at the heart of our storytelling, while inclusivity, diversity and equality are at the core of our thinking. Led by Co-Directors Caitríona McLaughlin (Artistic Director) and Mark O'Brien (Executive Director), the Abbey Theatre celebrates both the rich canon of Irish dramatic writing and the potential of future generations of Irish theatre artists.

Ireland has a rich history of theatre and playwriting and extraordinary actors, designers and directors. Artists are at the heart of our organisation, with Marina Carr and Conor McPherson as Senior Associate Playwrights and Caroline Byrne as Associate Director; and Esosa Ighodaro, John King, Lianne O'Shea and James Riordan as Resident Directors.

Our stories teach us what it is to belong, what it is to be excluded and to exclude. Artistically our programme is built on twin impulses, and around two questions: 'who we were, and who are we now?' We interrogate our classical canon with an urgency about what makes it speak to this moment. On our stages we find and champion new voices and new ways of seeing; our purpose – to identify combinations of characters we are yet to meet, having conversations we are yet to hear.

www.abbeytheatre.ie

ABBEY THEATRE SUPPORTERS

PROGRAMME PARTNER

CORPORATE GUARDIANS

Bloomberg

RETAIL PARTNER
ARNOTTS

GOLD AMBASSADORS

HOSPITALITY PARTNER
THE WESTBURY
THE DOYLE COLLECTION · DUBLIN

IT PARTNER

SILVER AMBASSADORS

interpath   ODGERS BERNDTSON

RESTAURANT PARTNERS

  Rosa Madre Restaurant

HAWKSMOOR

PLATINUM PATRONS
The Cielinski Family
Deirdre and Irial Finan
Sheelagh O'Neill
Carmel and Martin Naughton

DIRECTORS' CIRCLE PATRONS
Tony Ahearne
Pat and Kate Butler
Janice Flynn
Susan and Denis Tinsley
Elizabeth and Masoud Papp Kamali
in memory of Lloyd Weinreb R.I.P.
Donal Moore R.I.P.

SILVER PATRONS
Frances Britton
Tommy Gibbons
Andrew Mackey
Eugenie Mackey
Eugene Magee
Gerard and Liv McNaughton
Andrew and Delyth Parkes

Thank you to all the above supporters for your continued support of your national theatre.

Your generosity is key to creating a home for Ireland's theatre makers, players and dreamers in the national theatre. Support experiences like the one you've just seen at the Abbey Theatre today by making a donation to the productions of tomorrow.

Scan the QR code to donate.

Children of the Sun

Characters

Protasov, *a scientist*
Elena, *his wife*
Lisa, *Protasov's sister*
Chepurnoy, *a local vet*
Melania, *the vet's widowed sister*
Vagin, *a visiting photographer*
Yegor, *a handyman*
Misha, *the landlord's son*
Lusha, *a maid*
Troshin, *a stranger*
Roman, *a yard boy*

Setting

Act 1. *A large house in the country that has seen better days.*
Act 2. *A barren landscape.*

/ indicates next line to begin.
// indicates self-interruption.

Act One

One

Protasov *is alone. He sits looking at the sun, wearing swimming goggles.*

Lusha *approaches holding a petri dish and licking her fingers. She looks at the sun, then back at* **Protasov.**

Protasov *notices her.*

Protasov   I've forgotten your name.

Lusha   Lusha. The new girl.

Protasov   Lusha, the new girl! Splendid. I, Lusha, am ready for my lunch.

Lusha *looks sceptical.*

Protasov   Where are you from, Lusha?

Lusha   Kaluga.

Protasov   Ah-ha. Kaluga. Can't say I'm familiar with Kaluga.

Lusha   Not many people are.

Protasov   I've been looking at the sun, Lusha. You see, at the most infantile, most volatile moments of the universe, a clear cosmological signature was left for us to decipher. All we long to know, Lusha, written on gravitational waves, in temperature variations, on the muddied face of radiation. The entire picture painted on the sun and when we develop the capacity to see it, Lusha from Kaluga, we will observe a masterpiece.

Lusha   Those are swimming goggles, professor. You'll blind yourself looking at the sun in those.

Protasov *(removing goggles)*   Are you literate, Lusha?

Lusha   I know my prayers.

Protasov   We are simple folk here, Lusha. You'll relish your time with us. It's all quite amusing. Yes. Quite amusing.

(*Looks at her.*) You appear, Lusha, to be dining on the contents of my petri dish.

Lusha   I do?

Protasov   Is it . . . nice?

Lusha   Sweet.

Two

Morning. Sunlight.

Stairways. A domed glasshouse, full of curated exotic plants and trees, looking out over a flat expanse. Glass cases with exhibits and beautiful old scientific instruments. An area that is clearly **Protasov**'s *lair, like Prospero's cell.*

The stage is constantly populated. Characters pass through scenes, shifting the action to various levels.

The place is lush, finely wrought, and has the look of the great nineteenth-century botanical houses – but the characters are dressed in a way that might suggest early twentieth century. Or now.

Lisa *looks out through glass at* **Roman**, *young, vigorous, who is piling up mounds of red earth to form a ridge, a gash across the horizon.* **Lisa** *watches him from the top of the stairs. He looks up at her occasionally.*

On an upper level the photographer **Vagin** *works with lights and equipment. His cameras are vintage, box cameras etc, and the lights are like old film-set lamps. His clothes suggest the latter half of the twentieth century.*

Enter **Elena** *with milk and pills.*

Elena   What is he doing?

Protasov   Landlord's orders. Tell him to go away, will you? I'm struggling to think.

Elena   This heat. You'll suffocate on thinking. What is that smell in here?

Protasov   Don't open / the door.

Elena   Where's that stench coming from? Hello. Will you be much longer?

Roman *stares at her, she retreats.* **Lisa** *holds his gaze.*

Elena   That's bad, Pavel, rancid. What is it?

Protasov   The burner, in my study. I've had to vacate while the air clears. I need to speak to Yegor. You seen him?

Elena   Yes I have, unfortunately.

Protasov   What? Elena?

Elena   Been beating his wife again.

Protasov   Right. Right. Yes. Thing is, I need him to build me a burner, smaller, conical-shaped with / a hole on top

Elena   Speak to him. Can't you?

Protasov   Couldn't you?

Elena   He'll listen to you.

Protasov   You know I don't like confrontation, Elena. It disturbs my equilibrium.

Lisa (*descending stairs*)   Has he gone now? The yard-boy, has he gone?

Protasov   No, he has not gone.

Elena   Time for your milk, Lizonica.

Lisa   What is that smell?

Elena   Your milk, Lisa.

Lisa   I've watched him from my window all morning. What's he digging?

Protasov   A hole.

Lisa   A hole for what?

Protasov   For the sake of it?

Elena   Lisa!

Lisa   The soil is red.

Protasov   Is it?

Elena   Don't be silly.

Lisa   The soil is red. I don't like it.

Roman *straightens up, looks frankly at* **Lisa** *through the glass.*

Elena   It's soil, Lisa. It's to be neither liked nor disliked.

Lisa   Why is he here?

Protasov   Landlord's orders.

Lisa   I'm telling you, the soil is red.

Protasov   Do you think he might finally run out of it?

Elena   Lisa, please.

Lisa   At the end of the day, before sleep, write down three things that inspire gratitude.

The cat.

My two strong legs.

The blue jug by my bed.

Elena   What are you talking about?

Lisa   At the sanitorium they unstrapped me and spoke about gratitude. Their prescription: to write down, every night before sleep, three things I am grateful for.

The blue jug holds warm milk.

His blood washed out of my coat.

I was not bayoneted or shot through the chest.

Elena   Look at me, Lisa. I am not in the mood for time travel. I need you to stay in the here and now. The here and now, Lisa, is more than enough to manage.

Lisa   The here and now? You sure?

Roman *appears at the window. Sound of gunfire (First World War artillery).*

Elena   Your eyes are clear and calm, Lisa. Nice to see. Keep them that way.

Lisa   You speak to me like I'm a sick child.

Elena   Only when you behave like one.

Lisa   The doctor recommended sex, to soothe my nerves.

Protasov *(retreating to his lair)*   I'm sure I had an extended nozzle somewhere /

Elena   What doctor?

Lisa   My prescription: to become a tidy wife engaged in regular marital relations. Preferably with a husband in possession of an even temper and all his own teeth.

Elena   Difficult to pick up one of those in the pharmacy.

Lisa   What's it like?

Elena   What's what like?

Lisa   Marital sex.

Elena   River fish are bloated. Had you heard? Our neighbours think Pavel has poisoned the water.

Lisa   This has nothing to do with Pavel.

Elena   No.

Lisa   Last night I went to the Arctic, to the White Sea Canal. There are bodies there, thousands of them, buried in the walls, blocking up the sluices.

Elena   You spent last night in your bed. Take a pill.

Lisa   I took a pill.

Elena   You're going to need to steady up, Lisa. Stand on your own two feet.

(*Referring to* **Protasov**.) Both of you.

Lisa   Growing up here didn't really prepare my brother or me for life beyond these walls. I wonder sometimes if we're fully human or some kind of complicated algae clinging to the furniture.

Beat.

Elena   Have you considered the vet?

Lisa   To have sex with?

Elena   To look after you, Lisa, soothe your nerves.

Lisa   No, Elena, I have not considered the vet.

Elena   Shame. I'm sure he'd appreciate some human interaction, given that he spends a not insignificant amount of his time up to his elbows in quadrupedal mammals.

Lisa   To shag the vet or have my teeth knocked out in a psychiatric hospital?

Elena   It's a dilemma all right.

Lisa   Have *you*?

Elena   What?

Lisa   Considered the vet.

Elena   Where is Pavel?

Lisa   Have you?

Elena   I'm a married woman, Lisa, with far more pressing concerns. I don't have time to lie around fantasising about a rural vet.

Lisa   Don't you?

Elena   Maybe you'd like to look into your crystal ball, Lisa, and tell me what I'm supposed to do now. Maybe you'd like to ask the phantasmagoria how I am going to hold on to this house and take care of your brother.

Lisa   Do you love Pavel?

Elena   I have devoted my life to him.

Lisa   That wasn't what I asked.

Lisa *accepts milk and pill, swallows.* **Protasov** *joins them.*

Elena   I was just telling Lisa that you'll have to fend for yourselves today.

Protasov   Oh?

Lisa   I foresee destruction, Elena, not how to survive it.

Elena   The new girl is running things singlehanded.

Protasov   Will I have to make my own lunch?

Elena   Are you capable of making your own lunch?

Protasov   I have no idea.

Elena   Well then, let's hope she has some culinary skill. Get dressed today, Lisa, get some air.

Protasov   And Yegor?

Elena   Yegor?

Protasov   Before you go? Could you? Can't get a thing done without him.

Elena   I fetch him, you'll speak to him?

Protasov   If I must.

Elena (*exits*)   Air. Lisa.

Lisa   Speak to Yegor about what?

Protasov   Beating his wife again. Apparently.

Lisa   What'll you say?

Protasov (*preoccupied with burner part*)   Desist? Stop? Find a new hobby?

Don't you have anything to do today, Lisa? Some sprites to appease? Some nag to whisper to?

Lisa   You love Elena, don't you, Pavel?

Protasov   Yes, I love my wife. Wives are, on the whole, lovable.

Lisa *picks up burner part.*

Protasov   Please don't, it's / already

Lisa   I wouldn't be remotely lovable. I'd be exhausting.

Protasov   Indeed. Well, much as I enjoy our little chats / I do have work to do.

Lisa   Is Elena going to pose for Vagin today?

Protasov   'Do you love your wife?' 'Is she going to pose for Vagin?' Is this a parlour game?

Lisa   Is she?

Protasov   She's sitting for a portrait.

Lisa   You do know you pay her too little attention?

Protasov   And is Elena mute? If things are a little // if she occasionally feels // if some aspects of the marriage are // My wife can speak, can't she? She can speak for herself.

Beat.

For your information, Lisa, Vagin is not only a photographer of some renown, he has also become, since he came to stay, all that time ago, a very very good friend.

Lisa   Well, that makes all the difference.

Yegor *enters, sees* **Roman** *digging outside, goes straight to glass door.*

Protasov   Aha! Yegor! Terrific! My sister was just leaving.

Yegor   Roman! He is here.

Protasov   Yes, yes, he's been here all morning.

Yegor (*at door*)   Roman! My man!

Protasov   The thing is, Yegor, I need you to build me a burner, smaller, with a lid.

Yegor   Roman!

(*To* **Protasov**.) Roman is digging a hole.

Protasov   Indeed he is, and a fine hole it is too. The thing / is

Yegor   Big hole, hah? Deep.

Protasov   Indeed. The thing is, Yegor, I need a burner / conical-shaped, lidded.

Yegor (*going outside*)   Eh! Roman! Watch out! The vet's coming.

Roman *grins.*

Protasov   Oh really? What now?

Yegor   The vet's coming to have a look at your hole, what!

Protasov   Yegor! Yegor! Could you come inside? / I need

Lisa   Wife!

Protasov   What?

Lisa   You need to talk to him about his wife.

Enter **Chepurnoy**.

Chepurnoy   What wife? I don't have a wife.

Protasov   Yegor!

Chepurnoy   Some hole he's digging.

Protasov   Why are you here?

Chepurnoy   I come bearing gifts.

Protasov   Really? Could you dispense them quickly, I'm trying to get some work //

Yegor, might you come back?

Chepurnoy (*stench*)   Something cooking . . . small child perhaps?

Lisa   Hello.

Chepurnoy   Hello. You're home.

Lisa   Am I ever anywhere else?

Chepurnoy (*smelling air*)   Brewing potions, is he?

Lisa   Burning them more like. My brother is in a very great hurry to prove that we all exist in different dimensions. He believes that there are concurrent selves, out there somewhere, making the decisions we fail to make, that every unturned corner, every alternative impulse, every abandoned thought, is manifest, spinning out in the stratosphere.

Do you exist in other dimensions, vet, do you think?

Chepurnoy   Hope not. I'm barely managing the current iteration.

Lisa   Where you coming from?

Chepurnoy   Callout.

Lisa   Interesting?

Chepurnoy   Would you like it to be interesting?

Lisa   I could do with a little distraction, yes.

Chepurnoy   Well, this morning while you were sleeping in your fetid bed . . .

Lisa   What do you know about my bed?

Chepurnoy   I was called to a fine house in the town suffused with stuffed carp and sacred hearts, wherein a maid – timid girl with sharp little teeth – did squeeze in the door the tail of a dog.

Lisa   Did she indeed?

Chepurnoy   The dog, however, was no ordinary dog, belonging, as it does, to the wife of the town's most senior civil servant.

Lisa   Oh dear.

Chepurnoy   Oh dear is right. Door slammed, dog yelped, maid scarpered, and I was called, at great haste, to bandage the throbbing tail – and given, for my expertise, twenty smackers.

Lisa   A princely sum.

Chepurnoy   From a princely dog. I'd have bought you chocolate mice or Wellington boots, but I suspect the cash might have more urgent uses. Elena around?

Lisa   I don't need your money, vet.

Chepurnoy   No?

Lisa   What have I got to spend it on?

Chepurnoy   Get out, shall we, get some air? Lisa?

Lisa   What of the maid? Clumsy girl, sharp little teeth?

Chepurnoy   I left her cowering in the yard, waiting for retribution, the dog's yelps resounding in her tiny, rather lovely ears.

Lisa   I don't like your stories very much.

Chepurnoy   No?

Lisa   They're brutal.

Chepurnoy   Hardly.

Lisa   The soil is red. Do you see?

Chepurnoy   Come outside, Lisa. Find shade.

Lisa   The yard-boy, Roman. He's so dark, with his huge, offended eyes.

Chepurnoy   Suffocating in here.

Lisa   I've seen those eyes before.

Chepurnoy   Lisa /

Lisa   I see the red earth and the horror is resurrected in my soul. The crowd. Blood on their faces, blood on the sand. A boy at my feet, his face turned to me, his eyes so dark. He opens his mouth, tries to tell me his name. Hoof. Rifle. Bayonet. Surge. I lose him. He is lost.

Haven't you seen him? That boy. Haven't you seen that boy before?

Chepurnoy   Boys die all the time, in every fucking hellhole on earth. Life is a geographical Russian roulette, Lisa. Outside. Come on.

Lisa (*lightly*)   A new and more terrible plague is coming, yet, that will desolate all lands as it passes through.

Chepurnoy   Glad I called.

Lisa   A pestilence which walketh in darkness.

Chepurnoy   Wanna take a walketh with it?

Lisa   The hens are sick.

Chepurnoy   Mites. I'll take a look.

Lisa   The dogs are vomiting.

Chepurnoy   Dogs like vomiting. Second helpings. So, is Elena around?

Lisa   Do horses vomit?

Chepurnoy   No. Why?

Lisa   Elena's going to the smokehouse to pose for Vagin.

Chepurnoy   He's still here, is he?

Lisa   He's received a commission fee to produce a portrait collection.

Chepurnoy   Shame, that.

Lisa   'Dead World, Destitute Elites.' He's already photographed the old girl up in the keep, eating cat food under her medieval tapestries. Beef in gravy. Did Elena ask you to babysit me?

Chepurnoy   Nope.

Lisa   Keep an eye on me?

Chepurnoy   Nope.

Lisa   You have a life to live, vet. Cows to inseminate. Cats to neuter. You shouldn't be sent to nurse me. It's not dignified – you're a man of the world.

Chepurnoy   And what a world. The hens inside?

Lisa   Elena thinks I need a playmate.

Chepurnoy   I'm hardly the most obvious candidate.

Lisa   She fears my thinking is infectious. 'If we all allowed ourselves to feel the brutality of this world, Lisa, we'd be on our knees. The work of men would become meaningless.' Imagine, vet, essential world-turning, tail-bandaging, potion-cooking, portrait-making work could cease. What then of bruised dogs and weeping maids and the indignant wives of most senior civil servants, let alone the rest of us?

Chepurnoy   Come outside, Lisa. Get some air.

(*Stench.*) What is that man brewing?

Lisa (*looking out through glass*)   Roman has his hole to dig, Yegor his wife to beat. My brother has his science, you your injured beasts, myself included. Elena manages the money and the milk and her wearying beauty and her empty larder. Vagin has his lurid art and silver bangles. And I, vet, I am a fly trapped behind the glass.

Chepurnoy (*opens glass door*)   It's hot. I'll drive you to town, buy you an ice cream.

Lisa   Might rain.

Chepurnoy   It's a heatwave, Lisa.

Lisa   I have a duty to remain.

Chepurnoy   A duty to what?

Troshin *enters, speaking soundlessly.* **Lisa** *watches him.* **Chepurnoy** *doesn't see him.*

Lisa   My visions.

Troshin *perches at a bar.* **Lisa** *sits with him. It isn't clear whether he is aware of her, but he probably isn't – he may be in a different place.* **Lisa** *will see these glimpses of people and stories intermittently throughout the first half of the play.*

Yegor   Give me a ten pound note.

Protasov   Ten pound note? Yes, right.

(*Searching his pockets.*) Lisa, do you happen to / have?

Lisa   Elena minds the money.

Protasov   Right.

Lisa   He's got two of them.

Protasov   Give them here.

Lisa *puts her hand out for the cash.* **Chepurnoy** *reluctantly hands it over.*

Protasov   Will two ten pound notes do, Yegor?

Yegor   Two will do nicely. Thank you. Goodbye.

Protasov   And you'll return with the burner?

Yegor   Wild horses wouldn't stop me.

Protasov   Wonderful!

Lisa   Pavel.

(*Silently mouthing the word.*) Wife. . .

Protasov   Oh right. Yes. Yegor, before you // Could I have a word? My wife has asked, indeed insisted, that I speak to you.

Yegor   What about?

Protasov   It seems // how should I put it? // There is evidence to suggest that you're, goodness, beating your wife. Again. Maybe. Possibly. Or possibly not! Could all be a misunderstanding. Of course. That's what it is. A misunderstanding. Forgive me, Yegor, it's nothing. You're a busy man. I shall await your return with excited impatience!

Yegor   I am.

Protasov   You are?

Yegor   I am.

Protasov   Beating your wife?

Yegor   Regularly. Thoroughly.

Protasov   You do know, Yegor, intelligent man that you are, that is brutality?

Yegor   Brutality?

Protasov   Yes.

Yegor   Brutality is necessary. No? Like breath.

Protasov   Not // You might need to reconsider that.

Yegor *looks blankly at* **Protasov**.

Protasov   You, Yegor, are a human being, a conscious, sensate creature, the most beautiful being on earth.

Yegor   The most beautiful being on earth? Me?

Protasov   Metaphorically speaking, yes. Yegor, a person mustn't beat another person. It's unpleasant, unnecessary.

Yegor   Ask me first what I beat her for.

Protasov   Beating one's wife is unreasonable, my friend, dare I say uncivilised.

Yegor   I was beaten. All my life. Didn't do me any harm. My wife, maybe she is not a beautiful human full of light. Maybe she is the devil.

Protasov   Nonsense! Yegor! What is a devil?

Yegor   You, an educated man, ask me what is a devil? You, with your physicstry, your laboratory, your chemistry of smells, ask me what evil is?

Protasov   Annatonya is not evil. She's //

Yegor   Yes?

Protasov   A little beleaguered maybe?

Yegor   Is that right? A little beleaguered maybe, says the man taking orders from his wife.

Protasov   I'm not taking orders from my // I'm simply

Yegor   Think your father would have taken orders from a woman?

Protasov   My father didn't deem it necessary to follow any dictates but his own.

Yegor   You're a child.

Protasov   I am not a child. No. No, I am not a child.

Yegor   A wart on his palm.

Protasov   I think, actually, Yegor, my father meant that term affectionately.

Yegor   I will beat my wife. I will beat her until she bends before me like grass before the wind. I will beat her because she is my wife. She exists because I allow her to exist.

Yegor *exits.*

Protasov (*following him*)   Good, well, glad we got a chance to // About my burner, Yegor // Wait!

Protasov *exits.*

Chepurnoy   That went well. Personally, I'd have grabbed him by the eloquence and beaten him with a stick! Saved myself twenty quid.

Elena   Yegor's been, has he? // Vet. Personal or professional call?

Chepurnoy   Certainly not professional.

Elena   Oh good, we can't afford your fee. Heading out for a walk with the vet, Lisa? Wonderful. Maybe look in on the hens?

Lisa   I don't need to be managed, Elena.

Elena   Of course not. Of course you don't.

Chepurnoy   Front gates – your landlord has amassed a delegation of heavy machinery.

Elena   Really? And it's not even my birthday.

Chepurnoy   You're going to have to go. Vacate.

Elena   Thank you for your input.

Chepurnoy   My offer stands.

Lisa *goes outside, watches* **Roman**.

Chepurnoy   Come away with me, Elena. Now.

Elena   How?

Chepurnoy   Just walk out the door, Elena. Just walk.

Elena   And what, vet, do you suggest I do with my husband?

Chepurnoy   The last time I looked, my sweet, you weren't joined at the hip.

Protasov *holds broken burner.*

Chepurnoy   I see Yegor's wife came back?

Elena   Annatonya. Yes. She never quite seems able to walk away.

Chepurnoy   We'll take a stroll, check on the hens.

Chepurnoy *goes outside, reaches the ridge, looks into it, looks away, comes back to* **Lisa**, *keeps looking at* **Elena**.

Protasov   As I no longer have a working burner, the immediate, medium- or long-term prospect of having a working burner, I want boiling water for my glass.

Elena   Kettle's on the hob.

Protasov   I want boiling water, Elena. Get me boiling water!

Elena   Did you speak to Yegor?

Protasov   Left him shaking in his boots.

Elena   What did he say?

Protasov   What did he say? Let me see. He said that I was a child, you a meddlesome, ball-breaking fool and my father a saint, before cantering away with my twenty quid in his pocket.

Elena   Where did you get twenty quid?

Protasov   I want boiling water, Elena!

Elena   Stop it.

Protasov   Get me boiling water. Now!

Elena   Get it yourself, Pavel.

Protasov   Get it!

Elena   Tell the girl to get it.

Protasov   I don't want her anywhere near my study. Where did you find her? She's feral. Caught her licking out a petri dish.

Elena   Speak to her.

Protasov   Speak to her? Speak to her! I'm worn out speaking to people on your behalf. Yegor beating his wife! What business is it of mine? How do I know what people enjoy in the dungeons of their marriage? It is not my concern.

Elena   He's your employee, it is your concern.

Protasov   I am trying to think, Elena. Yes? I'm simply trying to think in this . . . this metropolis of need.

Elena   This metropolis of need? There's nobody here, Pavel. Look around you. Everybody's gone.

Protasov   Good! I never wanted them here in the first place.

Elena   Yes, well, you made that perfectly clear to my guests.

Protasov   Guests! Leeches.

Elena   My guests! My paying guests! My artists.

Protasov   Amateurs!

Elena   Amateurs or not, there's no one left here but Vagin. Artists' retreat? They've retreated so far they're specks on the horizon.

Protasov   For Christ's sake, Elena, how many ekphrastic poets can one man be expected to applaud in a lifetime? Tell me that.

Elena   They paid our rent.

Protasov   They exhausted me! I have work to do. Important, lasting work, and they exhausted me!

Elena   Your students /

Protasov   Different matter entirely.

Elena   They paid. The Dutch boy, Arie? Is he coming back?

Protasov   His research into liquid propellants attracted significant funding elsewhere. They all want to rocket to Mars. Arie was no different. We parted company.

Elena   I'm late.

Protasov   Anyone else you'd like me to lecture on their behaviour before you go? Yes? No? Couple of lascivious cats hanging around the scullery you'd like me to chastise? A slovenly mouse in your larder?

Elena   The radiator pump is dead.

Protasov   Replace it.

Elena   How, Pavel? With what?

Protasov   There's no money to heat the house, yet you go around opening all the windows and doors.

Elena   It's hot.

Protasov   Exactly!

Elena   Hot is an anomaly in this country.

Protasov   Have you read about atmospheric carbon dioxide?

Elena   I have to go.

Protasov   The world is overheating, Elena, a situation which does rather put your domestic pump predicament in the shade.

Elena   *My* predicament? We have to talk / Pavel

Protasov   I need boiling water. I don't want to talk to you about anything but boiling water.

Elena   This house is gone. We've lost it. The landlord has his machinery at the gate. They're going to level it. Everything.

Pavel   I thought Vagin was expecting you in the smokehouse. Mustn't keep the talent waiting.

Elena   He's paying me to sit for him.

Protasov   Well, lucky old you.

Pause. **Elena** *decides to go.*

Elena   There's cheese in the fridge.

Protasov   I suppose you'd like me to speak to it about its violent attitude towards the butter?

Protasov *becomes upset.* **Elena** *goes to him.*

Elena   Try to make sure Lisa eats something. Yes? And when Misha turns up looking for rent, tell him, tell him I'll speak to him later.

Protasov   Later, yes.

Elena   The hens are sick. They're not laying. They need to be kept inside.

Protasov   Inside, hens, yes. That is a lot of information, Elena.

Elena   Is it?

Protasov   Do you have any idea what I'm trying to achieve here, Elena?

Elena   Not really, Pavel. Not any more.

Protasov   I am attempting to colonise the last frontier. Time, Elena, time. The most valuable commodity on earth. I'm so close, Elena, so close. If we could inhabit different iterations of self, we could undo all the mistakes of the past and create something profoundly beautiful, Elena. Don't you see?

Elena   The hens – it's probably mites.

She goes to join **Vagin**, **Chepurnoy** *watches her.* **Lisa** *watches* **Chepurnoy**.

Protasov   The only velocity which exists, Elena, is the velocity of an object in relation to another object. Elena. Come back. Elena! Time, Elena, we need time. From a single cell to an entire plant, everything progresses, everything progresses.

Troshin *pilfers a few items from a glass case, disappears through the foliage.* **Lisa** *watches him.* **Melania** *knocks at the glass door.*

Protasov   Oh please! Please please please please please.

Melania   Anyone home?

Protasov   Melania.

Melania   Your door was left open.

Protasov   So I see.

Melania   This heat!

Protasov   Indeed.

Melania (*already inside*)   Deadening.

Protasov   You may as well come in.

Melania   Bit of a commotion at your gate.

Protasov   Oh yes?

Melania   Machines panting in the heat like big rusty dogs.

Protasov   Elena is dealing with it.

Melania   I'm not disturbing you, am I?

Protasov   Actually . . .

Melania   Yes?

Protasov   Actually, I'm not entirely displeased to see you, Melania.

Melania   Aren't you? That's a good start!

Protasov   I'd offer you tea, but I've been deserted. My wife, I asked her if she might bring boiling water before she left me. Outside of her remit. Unfortunately.

Melania   Unfortunately.

Protasov   So. Melania. You read the book?

Melania   Did I?

Protasov   The one I lent you?

Melania   Of course! Yes. All the . . . symbols.

Protasov   Formulas.

Melania   Formulas. Yes. Compelling. It's a little cooler over there – do you mind if I . . .?

Protasov   It's not a work of fiction.

Melania   It certainly is not.

Protasov   I thought you might enjoy the author's disregard for a universal and absolute parameter.

Melania   Did you?

Protasov   Daring.

Melania   Daring! You took the word right out of my mouth. Aren't you hot, Pavel? This heat . . .

Protasov   Deadening. You've said. Melania, may I ask you a personal question?

Melania   I wish you would.

Protasov   Do you have chickens?

Melania   Chickens?

Protasov   Poultry. Roosters. Hens.

Melania   Yes, I have poultry. I have roosters. I have hens.

Protasov   Wonderful.

Melania   Is it? Might I trouble you for a glass of water?

Protasov   So much is expected of me, Melania. I have work to do, essential scientific work, and still I am dragged down, denied, freighted by this . . .

Melania   This?

Protasov   Life.

Melania   I see it.

Protasov   My wife seems to think that I should spend my day telling people what's good for them and what's not. Yegor beating his wife. What can I do? What business is it of mine?

Melania   You really shouldn't be troubled by trivialities.

Protasov   And money!

Melania   Ah. Money.

Protasov   There is money or there is no money. It is not my responsibility.

Melania   No.

Protasov   People evaporate, reappear – farmer, landlord, priest. Never with what I need, always with demands.

Roman *looks through the window at* **Lisa**. *He moves away from the window, resumes his digging.* **Misha** *has been watching him. They disappear behind the hill of earth. On an upper level,* **Yegor** *dances* *silently.* **Lisa** *observes him.* **Chepurnoy** *focuses on* **Elena** *and* **Vagin**.

The sound of clocks, chiming and ticking at different intervals, drifts in quietly, as if on a breeze. The effect is magical, hypnotic.

Protasov   Let other people deal with them. Elena. Let her sort it out.

Melania   Absolutely.

Protasov   Endless. All of it. An endless distraction. I, Melania, am a man of science.

Melania (*mispronouncing the name*)   Like Pasteur.

Protasov   Pasteur?

Melania   Pasteur.

Protasov   Pasteur pioneered the study of molecular asymmetry in 1857!

Melania   Well, yes. Yes, obviously. I meant to say.

Protasov   Time, Melania. What is it?

Melania   It's a slippery customer, that's what it is.

Protasov   It's the last frontier. I want your eggs, Melania.

Melania   Do you? Really?

Protasov   Do you believe in chemistry, Melania?

Melania   Oh yes. Yes I do.

Melania *takes* **Protasov**'s *hand*.

Protasov   I have the most enthralling book to lend you. Promise me you'll study it.

Melania   A book! Another one? Goodness.

Protasov   Could I have my hand back?

Melania   Sorry?

Protasov   I've been experimenting. There may be a little contamination.

Melania   Contamination? Of course. Silly me.

Protasov   You smell eggs, Melania?

Melania   I didn't like to say.

Protasov   There is always risk with sulphuric acids. Dizziness, blurred vision, tightness in the chest, sweating, muscle twitching.

Melania   Tiresome but hardly fatal.

Protasov   Convulsions, fits, asphyxia, death.

Melania   Risk then.

Protasov   There is no progress without hazard.

Melania   None.

Pause. They are very close to each other. **Melania** *becomes a little overcome by the stench.*

Melania   Would it be inappropriate for me to ask, Pavel, what it is you're doing with sulphuric acid? In this weather?

Protasov   Iron filings and sulphur, heated in the burner until they start to glow /

Melania   Glow?

Protasov   . . . will, as any fool can tell you, create an exothermic reaction of the two elements iron and sulphur to form iron sulphide! Used, as I hardly need to tell you, in the preparation of hydrogen sulphate.

Melania   Is that right? Call me a fool, Pavel, I'm lost.

Protasov   Hair dye!

Melania   You're making hair dye?

Protasov   For my good friend Vagin, who is at this very moment preparing to render my wife.

Melania   Is that right?

Protasov   He prefers a particular tone of cobalt, he's a little sensitive on the subject.

Melania   He'd not just go to the hairdresser, no?

Protasov   Hardly.

Melania   Hardly.

Protasov   Pay attention to science, Melania, and you will see the eye of God in the mysteries of the structure of matter. Science stares bravely and precisely at the fiery mass of the sun, at the crust of the earth, at the secret structures of stones, at the silent life of a tree, at the invisible particles of the heart. Everywhere it casts its gaze, science discovers harmony.

Melania   That's beautiful, Pavel.

Protasov   My mother's words. Gifted amateur. A woman to inspire wonder. Sadly, Melania, my work is not so easily understood.

Melania   Time. The last frontier.

Protasov   I have lost my funding again. Once again fallen foul of the money men. Defence, agriculture, picnics on Mars. Just tiresome.

Melania   You must be heard beyond this backwater. I can help you, Pavel. I have the means. I can buy you silence. A laboratory. Two laboratories. Anything you ask for.

Protasov   You're too gracious.

Melania   When I listen to you, I want to kiss your hands.

She kisses his hands passionately. **Lusha** *watches, unseen.*

Protasov   Don't, Melania! You never know where they've been.

Melania   You want the flock, Pavel?

Protasov   Sorry?

Melania   Chickens. Roosters. Hens. You want my entire flock?

Protasov   Just the produce actually.

Melania   For your work?

Protasov   And an occasional omelette. If you could give me fresh, just-laid, still-warm eggs.

Melania   I'll send you a dozen every morning.

Protasov   Wonderful. And Melania . . .

Melania   Yes?

Protasov   Your remaining offers we might discuss at a more opportune time?

Beat.

Melania   Your wife, you mentioned, is currently being rendered?

Protasov   Yes. She's posing for Vagin in the smokehouse.

Melania   And you aren't afraid?

Protasov   What have I to be afraid of, Melania?

Melania   My late husband was an immensely wealthy man.

Protasov   It's well known.

Melania   A butcher, wholesale, by trade and by nature. And you, you are a child, laying out the invisible particles of the heart like toy soldiers in a marching line.

Protasov   I am not a child, Melania.

Melania   What might a butcher's widow do, do you think, when confronted with such tenderness? Purchase you. By the pound. Tongue. Heart. Shank. Hind.

Protasov   I should probably get back / to

Melania   Had I spent my days in the company of another man, Pavel Fyodorovich, my husband would have slit my throat.

Pause. The sound of the clocks has disappeared. **Protasov** *goes back to his books/experiments.* **Troshin** *takes his hat off to* **Lisa**.

Troshin   Pardon me, madame. Sans shoeses. Fortune is adverse, madame! I am tired. Tired, tired, tired, barely standing.

He drifts away. **Lisa** *stares at the space he has occupied.* **Yegor** *is at the bar.* **Lisa** *looks into his eyes; he doesn't see her.*

Elena *poses.* **Vagin** *adjusts light, looks at her from various angles. Time passes.*

Vagin   Now I know what to do with you. A contusion of yellows with one heliotrope breast.

Elena   A bruise?

Vagin   The work requires context if it's to be taken seriously. Open your mouth. More. My last project was all generational trauma, collective cultural memory. Bloodied babies washing up on the seashore. White-lipped girls shivering at ferry ports. This time, mouth. I want to injure privilege. Give me some riding-crop rage, Elena.

Elena   I don't own a riding crop.

Vagin   Disappointing. Think Pavel might pose in a pair of jodhpurs?

Elena   He's busy.

Vagin   Monstrous, the way that man ignores you.

Elena   My concerns are too blunt. I exhaust him.

Vagin   You should be free of him, Elena.

Elena   And what would I do with freedom, Dmitry? I've no training for it whatsoever. If he didn't need me / I

Vagin   Mouth.

Elena   If he didn't need me // I don't know. Who'll take care of him?

Vagin   He's a parasite. He'll find some other aperture to burrow into. Why you sacrifice yourself to that man is beyond me. Stop fidgeting.

Elena   He was a brilliant man, is a brilliant man. First time I ever saw him, I'd extracted myself from a party full of boors, one in particular. Pavel was alone, throwing up on a fire escape. I walked him home, he apologised all the way. We got to the door of his digs, sat on the freezing front step, looked at the stars, and he told me that we'd soon understand the conditions of a universe less than a trillionth of a second old. And if we understood our past, he said, we could understand our future. And I told him that his friends were mocking pigs and he said he had no friends, and it was almost light by then and on the street thin dogs and staunch women were starting their day. I told him to go to bed and that I'd come for him the next day . . .

Vagin   Sorry, I zoned out. What were you saying?

Elena   I was the one who decided he needed saving. He never asked. I was the one who decided he needed taking care of. I may not contribute much to this world, but at least I can try to //

Vagin   What?

Elena   Make retribution.

Vagin   Lisa and her grim prognosis have had a bad influence on you.

Elena   It's loathsome to cause Pavel more suffering. Degrading. He's already lost so much.

Vagin   Sing your song loudly and for yourself. That's my motto.

Elena   My father used to tell me that beauty was the only currency I'd ever need. I was never allowed show displeasure. Rage, he warned, would stretch my face like a fist in a calfskin glove, make me hideous.

Vagin   And what evidence does love leave?

Elena   Love he failed to mention.

Vagin   You're beautiful, Elena.

Elena   But?

Vagin   Beauty needs an element of strangeness. Simple, unintended, unconscious strangeness. Strangeness is what gives it the right to be called beauty. Reverse the proposition and try to imagine a commonplace beauty.

Elena   Did you think of that?

Vagin   God, no.

Elena *holds out her hand in front of her face.*

Elena   This is my hand.

Vagin   Yes.

Elena   You see it?

Vagin   Yes.

Elena   I cannot see my hand. It's nothing to me. Matter. But if you see my hand, then I can see what you see. Finger, freckle, tendon, bone, cuticle, band of gold. Imagine, if you care to, my grip.

Vagin   Elena . . .

Elena   I am a common beauty invisible to herself. Without your approval, without your gaze, I don't exist. There is nothing to see. Nothing of worth. That is the knowledge I sucked up from this wet earth. There's your bruise, Dmitry.

There is a small explosion from **Protasov**'s *bench.*

Melania   Show yourself!

Lusha   Ma'am.

Melania   You spying on me?

Lusha   No.

Melania   What were you doing?

Lusha   Polishing his petri dish. The hens are dying. Cupboards are bare. I used to work below in the convent. Sister Polycarp loved a biscuit. Are your hens laying, ma'am?

Melania   Why this obsession with my poultry?

Lusha   I could work for you. Collect your eggs. Crawl inside your henhouse, search in the dirt. Hold them in my palms. Carry them to you in my apron.

Melania   What's your name? No, never mind. There is something you can do for me. You notice anything untoward about your mistress, let me know.

Lusha   Untoward?

Melania   Suspicious.

(*Money.*) Here. There's more where that came from.

Lusha   How much more?

Melania   I'm going to the garden. My brother is there, is he?

Lusha   The vet is in attendance, yes.

Chepurnoy *is still hovering near* **Elena** *and* **Vagin**.

Melania   Universal and absolute parameter?

Chepurnoy   What?

Melania   Universal and absolute parameter? What is it?

Chepurnoy   You're asking *me*?

Melania   You're a vet, aren't you?

Chepurnoy   Precisely. I am a *vet*.

Melania (*exiting*)   You're infuriating.

Lusha *explores the room.* **Misha** *creeps up behind her, touches her. She reacts instantly, clouts him. He's thrown over a chair.* **Roman** *is at the window. He smiles, makes an obscene gesture at* **Lisa**. *There is the sound of distant bombings (including the whine of a Second World War V2 rocket).*

Misha   What the fuck? I was just being friendly.

Lusha   You're no friend of mine.

Misha   We haven't been introduced. I'm Misha, yeah? Landlord's son. Misha. And you are?

Lusha   Lusha. No relation to the landlord whatsoever.

Misha   Beware the Lusha, eh? Anyone ever said that to you before?

Lusha   No.

Misha   New, are you? Your predecessor got out while the going was good. You might think to follow her.

Lusha   Why would I do that?

Misha   Be a smart move to get out of this place.

Lusha   That right?

Misha   That's right. Place stinks. Smell it for miles.

Lusha   What's it smell like?

Misha   Shit.

Lusha   Do I smell like that?

Misha   Let me see. You smell like damp, sweet damp, sweat.

Lusha (*restraining him*)   Beware the Lusha, landlord's son.

Misha   Where you from, Lusha? Been a guest of the convent, have you? On the run from the Poor Little Sisters of the Divine Jaysus, are you?

Lusha   What's it to you?

Misha   What did they take from you, Lusha, eh?

Lusha *takes her time not answering. Sound of sniper fire in the distance.*

Misha   I'm thinking you might be looking for some new employment, Lusha. Me 'n' my Daddio plan to level this place, open ourselves a small industry.

Lusha   What kind of industry?

Misha   Given the historically observed, not inconsiderable openness of males, and indeed some unfortunate females, of all ages, to shelling out good money after bad to tackle the scourge of baldness, we're going for the hair restoration market.

Lusha   That right?

Misha   If you knew the money spent on hair products, many deleterious to the general health of the purchaser, their efficacy predicated on misinformation – case in point: ordinary baldness is not brought on by fever, gout, violent emotion, indigestion or the wearing of heavy headdresses – you, Lusha, would eat your hat.

Protasov *ignites something on his bench. The smell permeates the stage.*

Lusha   So what do you propose?

Misha   We, Lusha, are bringing a brand new machine to market. As reported to the Constantinople Medical Society, a machine designed to bore a hole in the scalp, in which we insert a hair, which sometimes takes root and grows.

Lusha   And how might I assist your enterprise?

Misha   Well, now that you ask.

Lusha   Back off!

Misha   I'm an educated man, Lusha, I understand commerce. Think about it. Hair restoration is just the beginning. Think pomades, think perfumes for the discerning man.

Lusha   I *am* thinking, Misha. I'm thinking about the value of my own commercial assets. Just like Sister Polycarp taught me.

Misha   She have any other good advice, the Mother Superior?

Lusha   Careful your patent leather party shoes don't reflect your knickers.

Misha   Bit too late for you, eh?

Lusha   I was thinking I'd like to get married.

Misha   Who's going to marry you, Lusha? Some peasant who beats you like Yegor beats his wife?

Lusha   I hear Kharpov the baker's single. Again.

Misha   Kharpov the baker! That old geezer will be knocking the air out of you seven nights a week. I'm offering to set you up in something modest, Lusha, clean. See you're fed, maybe even throw in a bit of education for you.

Lusha *begins cleaning.*

Protasov   You want to see me?

Misha   I do.

Protasov   Where's your father?

Misha   Unavoidably detained. Asked me to drop by.

Protasov   I assume this isn't a social call.

Misha   The rent wouldn't go amiss.

Protasov   Rent? When was it due?

Misha   Six months ago.

Protasov   Six months? Just six months! Yet still you choose to be indelicate. My wife deals with domestic circumstance.

(*To* **Lusha**.) Are you *cleaning*?

Lusha   That is what I do.

Protasov   Extraordinary. Try not to eat anything, will you?

Misha   Daddio's expressed an interest in your remaining land /

Protasov   Daddio's already got my land.

Misha   Your acre of river frontage. Wondering if it might be for sale.

Protasov   What idiot would buy it? It's just gorse and shale.

Misha   We're idiots. Sell it to us.

Protasov   What for?

Misha   We're in the business of expansion, me and my dad.

Protasov   How exhausting.

Misha   Dunno if Daddio mentioned it, but I myself am a recent graduate from the institute of commerce.

Protasov   He didn't.

Misha   I understand industry.

Protasov   Delighted to hear it. Goodbye.

Misha   My dad and I desire nothing more than to develop the local economy.

Protasov   You'll be closing your loan company then?

Misha   Hobby, that. Charity operation to help our neighbours. Male grooming. There's a world of opportunity

out there. Out there, the art of fragrance is the art of living
. . .

Protasov   Buy my land, expand away. You've got
everything else. Just do me the courtesy of buggering off
and letting me get on with my work.

Misha   Hold on! Details. Daddio will want the deets.

Sound of approaching conflict, still in the distance. **Yegor** *is drunk,
talking to himself.* **Lisa** *listens.*

Yegor   You're reading a book, I say. You're some genius,
she says, you figure that out all on your own? Give us the
book, I say. No, she says. No?

He springs away from the bar.

You! Call your master.

Lusha (*beginning to exit*)   Call him yourself.

Yegor   Do what you're fucking told. Tart.

Yegor *attempts to strike* **Lusha**. *She ducks. He catches her hair.*

Yegor   I said call your master! Slut!

Lusha   Let go of me. Get him off me!

Protasov *enters.*

Protasov   Yegor! Ah, Yegor! I thought I heard your voice.
You came back! Wonderful! Oh.

Yegor   I drank the vet's money. I can't speak when I'm
sober.

Protasov   Yegor. Good man. Let // Sorry, what's your name
again?

Lusha   Lusha!

Protasov   Let Lusha go.

Yegor   You offended me, Pavel Fyodorovich.

Melania, Chepurnoy *and* **Lisa** *start to pay attention.*

Protasov   Unintentionally, I'm sure.

Lisa *laughs.*

Yegor (*to* **Protasov**)   I thought you were my friend.

Protasov   Did you?

Yegor   The crows gather. Shoo them away, good Pavel Fyodorovich. I am not a kind man.

Lusha   Let me go!

Protasov   Yegor, unhand the girl. See reason.

Yegor   You hurt my feelings. You think I am an animal.

Melania   You *are* an animal, we're all animals.

Protasov   I don't think you're an animal, Yegor. I think you're a talented, if somewhat crude, craftsman. However, one is only a person when one is able to reason. Reason, Yegor, sets one free.

Yegor   You think I'm a brute. You've always thought me a brute.

Protasov   Let the maid go, Yegor. When one can reason, one is honest and kind! Kindness was created by reason! Without reason, there is no kindness.

Melania   That is eloquent.

Protasov   Thank you, Melania. Yegor?

Yegor (*to* **Protasov**)   I'm not a kind man. I have not known kind men.

Melania   There are remarkably few of them about.

Yegor   My grandfather beat me unconscious. Many, many times. Is that reasonable?

Protasov   No, no, that is not reasonable.

Yegor   Is that brutal?

Protasov   Yes, I fear it is.

Yegor   And if he beat me for my own sake, from the good of his heart, is that also brutal?

Protasov   I believe so, yes.

Yegor   That is where you are wrong. You're wrong! We all have lessons to learn. And I will teach my wife. She belongs to me. She is mine. I love her, and if she cannot love me in return then I will crush her.

Lusha   I'm not your fucking wife. Leave me go!

Protasov   Reason, Yegor! Remember what I told you before: you are a conscious, sensate creature . . .

Yegor   You call me beautiful, but you offend me.

Melania   Who's beautiful? What is he talking about?

Protasov   I was speaking metaphorically.

Melania   Pardon my French, but you were speaking through your arse.

Yegor   Speak from your heart, Pavel Fyodorovich. Tell me, am I a beautiful human?

Melania   Of course you're not, you fool. You're a bog-standard abomination.

Yegor   I am asking you, Pavel Protasov, am I loved? Tell me, man of science, am I loved? Why can she not love me? Tell me! Tell me! Do you want me to kneel in front of you? Do you? Do you?

Yegor *sinks to his knees.* **Lusha** *is released.*

Protasov   I'm sorry if I have offended you, Yegor.

(*Softly.*) Yegor . . .

Yegor   Yes?

Protasov   Now that you're here, might we discuss / my burner?

Yegor   I have been living offended since I was a child. Nobody loves me.

Sound of cannons in the distance.

Melania   Pull yourself together, man. You're alive, aren't you?

Yegor   I am alive? Is that it? I am alive.

Protasov   And everything is alive alongside you. Life, everywhere. Mysteries, everywhere. Human life dwells among deep secrets of being. Life, Yegor, can be a source of inexhaustible happiness and . . . beauty.

Yegor   Why, then, is my world so cruel?

Melania   Probably because you're a pig-ignorant wife beater.

Yegor   I respect you, Pavel Fyodorovich. I do. I see you are a special man, I can feel it. But you've already grown a beard. A bearded person cannot take orders from women.

Yegor *begins to exit, watched by* **Lisa**.

Protasov   Yegor! The burner . . .

Melania   Pavel Fyodorovich, you were magnificent! Mind you, you'll need another handyman, and unfortunately they're all drunks.

(*To* **Lusha**.) Are you going to stay on the floor all day, dear?

Protasov   I'm exhausted, absolutely exhausted.

Melania (*to* **Lisa**)   Looking a little peaky, sweetheart. Why don't you run along and take a pill?

Lisa *goes to* **Lusha**, *offers her her hand to get off the floor.* **Melania** *watches, then turns away.*

Lisa   Did you eat the soap?

Lusha   I might have.

Lisa *touches* **Lusha**'*s hair. There is an acknowledgement of the pain that* **Lusha** *is in.*

Lisa   After he took my mother away, my father, the General, used to sit me on his knee and plait my hair. Binding my mane, he called it. He'd bind my mane so tightly my scalp would burn.

Lusha   Did she ever come back? Your mother.

Lisa   To me, sometimes. He took her away one August. She'd been washing loganberries in the sink. He had the yard boy catch her from behind, load her onto the back seat. Pavel and I watched by the scullery door. She was entirely still. They drove away and Pavel climbed onto the draining board and lifted the sieve. We ate the loganberries, and when they were gone Pavel said we were to bite down on our fingers until they bled.

Lusha *leaves.*

Lisa *is by the glass wall.* **Roman** *is on the other side.* **Lisa** *places her hand on the glass, obscures his face.*

The sky darkens. We have moved into evening. **Chepurnoy** *has been drinking.* **Vagin**, *who has been searching for drink, arrives with bottles and a wheelchair. He pours drinks for everyone.*

Vagin   Art!

Chepurnoy   Chickens!

Vagin   Art has always belonged to the few. That is its pride.

Elena   That is its tragedy. Art must make people better.

Vagin   Art can have no goals.

Chepurnoy   Chickens! Descendants of dinosaurs /

Protasov (*to* **Vagin**)   My dear friend, there is nothing pointless in the world.

Vagin   Except for the world itself.

Chepurnoy   Chickens recognise up to a hundred faces, including humans. That's all of us and half the village. And what do we do? Shove a lemon up their arse and roast them.

Elena   Dmitry Sergeevich! Life is hard; a person can get tired of living. Life is vulgar. Beauty is rare, but when beauty is genuine it warms the soul, like the sun coming out on a gloomy day. It is necessary for all people to understand and love beauty. Then they will be able to build a whole ethic upon it. They will be compelled to judge their actions as beautiful or ugly. And then life will be wonderful!

Protasov   That is superb, Lena!

Lisa   It is meaningless, Lena.

Protasov   That will resonate beautifully in all your parallel existences, my darling.

Elena (*gets bottle, pours drink for* **Chepurnoy**)   Shall I be mother?

Lisa   Last night I went to the Arctic, to the White Sea Canal.

Elena   Absinthe poses a suicide risk apparently. They really should charge extra.

Vagin (*top up*)   Over here!

Lisa   There are bodies there, thousands of them, buried in the walls, blocking up the sluices.

Elena (*topping* **Vagin**'s *glass*)   Shush. Good girl.

Lisa   Their sockets were hollow. One by one they opened their mouths and spat out an eyeball.

Elena   Shush. Stop it.

Lisa   The dead are our witnesses, don't you see?

Chepurnoy (*grabbing* **Elena**'s *wrist and speaking directly to her*) I used to sleep. Now I lie awake. I no longer dream. I stare. I want to do something heroic. But what? How? And I have this vision of a little piglet floating down the river on a chunk of ice. Such a small, pink, perfect little piglet, squealing and squealing. And I jump into the river and save her. But she doesn't care, she has no interest in valour. And it's such a pity because I have no choice but to eat her myself with horseradish.

Elena   Sometimes I toss and turn /

Chepurnoy   Go on.

Vagin   Freud would say that the pig is symbolic of your mind's inability to control your instincts and desires, vet.

Chepurnoy (*still holding* **Elena**)   Tell your friend Freud, whoever he is, that I have no desire to control my instincts and desires. Elena Nikolaevna, marry me!

Elena (*breaking away*)   I'm already married, as far as I remember.

Lisa   The way you joke, sister, it's so grave and strange.

Elena   Marriage to your brother feels like an endless perambulation around the garden in very tight shoes and with an irritating itch. Which is not to say that I don't love him, dearly.

(*To* **Protasov**.) Don't I?

Protasov   What's that?

Elena   LOVE YOU DEARLY.

Protasov   Marvellous.

Elena   Sometimes I toss and turn /

Lisa   I try to pull open the sluice gates. But I can't. I can't.

Chepurnoy (*to* **Elena**)   You toss and turn. Please. Please go on. You toss and turn /

Elena   I toss and turn and imagine a painting. A ship, bowsprit pushing through a boundless sea, embraced by angry green waves, and on the prow strong, powerful people standing there with open, cheerful faces, smiling proudly, some with a tincture of sea foam on their chin, gazing straight ahead, ready to calmly perish on the way to meet their destiny and . . .

Protasov   And?

Elena   Sometimes, sometimes the people are walking under the scorching sun across a yellow desert. Proud, determined, simple people, the great unsung people who have helped us evolve from the animals and brought us closer to being humans! And . . .

Protasov   And?

Elena   I search for my own face among them, but never find it.

Protasov   But of course you're there! On the prow, possibly a little obscured by Darwin.

Elena   This morning I looked in the mirror. I looked into the mirror and the glass was blank.

Troshin *stands there unnoticed.*

Vagin   Elena Nikolaevna! There will be only one person at the front of the ship. She will have the face of the woman who has left all her hopes on the shore, her eyes alight with the fire of determination.

Protasov   To the sun! The source of life! Render it, Vagin! Render it.

Troshin   Dear sirs! I've been waiting for a long time for you to finish your conversation, but I must interrupt you, as simple as that!

Chepurnoy   What do you want?

Troshin   Let me introduce myself: Second Lieutenant Yakov Troshin, former deputy director of the logging station. That very Yakov Troshin whose wife and child were killed by the train. I've got more children but no more wife. And with whom have I the honour of speaking?

Vagin   Sober people talk in such a peculiar manner.

Troshin   Pardon me, monsieur. Sans shoeses. Fortune is adverse. I am tired, barely standing. A gentleman by the name of Yegor, gracious enough to extract me from a mephitic ditch, did infer he had a pair, in ill repair, which he might see his way to parting with.

Lisa   His quarters are by the gate. You passed them on your way here.

Troshin   Re-merci! I've been looking for him all day. Very tired. Very very tired, barely standing. By the gate, you say? What a generous world. So full of hope and sometimes offering a small libation? No? Not to be.

Elena   Stop it.

Troshin   Very very tired, barely standing.

Elena   Stop.

Troshin   Pardon me, madame. Sans shoeses.

Elena   Stop it. Stop speaking.

Troshin   Fortune is adverse, madame!

Elena   Go away. Go away, can't you?

Lisa   Here. Take it.

She gives him a bottle.

Troshin   What a generous world. A generous world.

Elena   We're having a party. Do you understand? We are people with faces in the mirror and shoes on our feet, talking about art. Art. And I don't suppose, poor fellow, you'd have anything at all to contribute. Would you?

Troshin   No. I don't suppose.

Elena   No.

Chepurnoy, *very drunk, gets out of his chair.*

Chepurnoy   I know you. Spectre. Fuck off back to where you came from.

Troshin   I think, sir, that you may be mistaking me for someone else.

Chepurnoy   Fuck off! Back to where you came from. Fuck off!

Troshin   Yakov Troshin knows his manners. Simple as that. Yakov Troshin bids you adieu!

Chepurnoy *moves ineffectually towards* **Troshin**. **Troshin**, *watching* **Elena**, *leaves. Throughout the next scene, the sound of distant conflict begins to become audible. A helicopter hovers.* **Protasov** *conducts an experiment, tipsy.*

Elena   Where were we?

Vagin   Making my way back from the smokehouse through the turbulent greenery, with the general's stash in his bath chair, I espied Sister Polycarp careering towards town on her bicycle.

Chepurnoy   Was Polycarp in possession of a chicken?

Vagin   No chicken, just an ancient nun riding side-saddle who gave me the finger and told me the world is ending, the mother house lost.

Elena   The tramp – has he gone?

Chepurnoy   Gone.

Elena   My father despised the poor. They terrified him. As if he caught some scent of himself /

Vagin   One can never fully understand the minds of the peasantry, Elena – excitable, easily distracted, marvellously unburdened by affairs of the mind. Come the full moon they'll all be rolling around with the beasties in the mugwort, whistling polkas through their gums.

Elena I should have offered him a drink //

Chepurnoy Fuck him.

Vagin Vet! Done something to your beard?

Chepurnoy Nope.

Vagin Must be the light.

Elena There is nothing left, is there? Nothing.

Vagin *photographs* **Chepurnoy**. **Melania** *swings in with a gun*.

Melania Exchequer civil servant insisted I take this thing when I was leaving. Said the place was rotten with the angry and the dispossessed, even here in our little neck of the woods! Never know what they might do to a woman alone, he said. Mad as a box of frogs, that man. Eyeballs all over the walls, not to mention my décolletage – pardon my French.

Vagin Voracious man, the exchequer civil servant. Disturbingly tiny wife. Know him, vet? Mouth!

Snap.

Chepurnoy I had a passing acquaintanceship with his pointer.

(*To* **Elena**.) Come away with me.

Vagin In my role as artistic adviser to the rich and tasteless /

Chepurnoy That's a role, is it?

Vagin Darling, a talent as paltry as mine requires ingenuity to make it stretch.

Elena Where is Pavel? Lisa?

Lisa Pavel has work to do.

Vagin   In my role as artistic adviser to the rich and tasteless, I had the exchequer civil servant decorate his entrance hall with rows of individually framed prosthetic eyeballs. Elena! Tell the vet about the eyeballs.

Elena   Art, apparently.

Vagin   Of course it's art. Left to his own devices, the man would festoon the place with portraits of his unprepossessing ancestry. We need glasses. Where's the girl?

Chepurnoy   I once castrated a ram with testes the size of cannonballs. If I'd known it was art, I'd've framed them. Elena?

Vagin   Standards, Elena! Glasses?

Elena   There is no money.

Chepurnoy   The eyeballs are art, are they, Dmitry?

Chepurnoy *drinks by the neck.*

Vagin   The eyeballs have impact.

Elena   The eyeballs are meaningless.

Vagin   Art is whatever we decide it is.

Chepurnoy   Who's we?

Elena   We are all we.

Vagin   We are certainly not all we. Art belongs to the few. That is its pride.

Elena   Or its tragedy.

Vagin   Art should challenge, disturb. That sun is sullenly over the yardarm. Where is the girl? Ring, Elena. Ring!

Chepurnoy   Let me help you.

Elena *hesitates, then nods in agreement.*

There is a small explosion. The smell permeates the space.

Vagin   Ring! Elena.

Elena   Ring what, Dmitry?

Vagin   Ring something.

Elena   If art has any purpose, it should make us feel better.

Vagin   Better? Better? Do not for one moment, Elena, conflate the produce of Sunday painters, easels festooned with groaning viaducts, with art, Elena. Similarly, foisting lumbering still-lifes of over-ripe fruit bowls on one's friends and relatives should incur stiff penalties. I'm talking about art, Elena! Art and sex. Both should make us feel fantastically worse!

(*Roaring.*) Can somebody bring me a glass!

Elena   I thought art was to console those broken by life.

Protasov *looks defeated, his hands red.*

Elena   But then maybe some of us are beyond consolation.

Vagin (*bottle*)   Didn't happen to fish another one of these out of your crucible, did you?

Protasov   The chickens are dead, Elena. What was it you told me to do?

Elena   What happened to your hands?

Protasov   I buried the chickens.

Vagin   Should've said. I could've captured you on your knees in the red earth.

Lisa   Red. He sees it.

Chepurnoy   We all see it.

Lisa   None of you see anything.

Vagin   Have a drink, man. We're discussing art. Your wife is insisting that art should make us feel better.

Protasov   Better about what?

Elena   Pavel?

Protasov   Lusha tried to wash my // The dogs are still, Elena, far too still. I haven't been having the best of days, Elena. Who is the master of this house, I ask myself. Who? I don't know. I'm so busy, Elena, and Lisa is a sick person and you are away all day long, my darling Elena. All day. What difference if this house is abandoned, if we all go without the attention we // You were made for a beautiful life, my sweet. I'm not so blind as not to see that. I said to myself, 'Elena was made for a beautiful life'.

Elena, *in a sudden fit of impotent temper, takes one of* **Protasov**'s *instruments and smashes it against the floor/wall. Pause. Change of mood.*

Elena (*whispered*)   I'm sorry. I'm sorry I'm sorry I'm sorry.

Chepurnoy   I took a boy in off the street once. An urchin. Utterly silent. At night he danced around my rooms to a music of his own. A wild agitation, twirling, leaping. When I restrained him, which I often did, he'd break free of me and smash his delicate head against the walls.

Lisa   What happened to him?

Chepurnoy   In the end I let him go. Took in a girl. Young. Thought I might marry her. She stabbed me.

Melania   My brother doesn't love me. We're strangers. He was raised in Poltava by our maiden aunt; I was sent to Yaroslavl, to our uncle's. We're orphans.

Chepurnoy   Which we never hesitate to mention.

Melania   My brother is desperate for someone to love him, even an urchin boy. His life hasn't turned out like he wanted. A rural vet. Saw himself as an artist, settling old scores with the depth of his insights. Putting all that boyhood pain to some use. Didn't you, Boris?

Chepurnoy   Veterinary skills came in handy once you'd married the butcher, Melania. Deep wounds to suture. We should've gelded the old bastard on sight.

Melania   You live and learn.

Chepurnoy (*pouring* **Melania** *a drink*)   Married at twenty, nearly killed herself from sadness and disgust. Eh, Melania? Drank ammonia.

Melania   Drank ammonia! I'd forgotten that.

Elena   Forgotten? Why did you marry him?

Melania   Where else was I going to go? My uncle was finished with me. I was sold. Tried to hang myself. Twice!

Chepurnoy   First time I cut you down.

Melania   Second time my husband tore me down.

Chepurnoy   I should've killed him.

Melania   You did your best. He died of gout in the end. Agonisingly. Cheers.

Elena *reluctantly raises her glass.*

Melania (*to* **Elena**)   Your husband – if you heard how he spoke to me. Me, Melania Kirpicheva! For the first time in my life, somebody spoke to me about miracles. I'm not saying I understood him, but when you live as I have lived, as if in a terrible dream, and someone opens your eyes and it's morning // Well, he won't be lingering on the shelf.

Elena   I don't always enjoy honesty, Melania, it's a blunt tool capable of destroying conversation. However, if we are to be friendly, I am going to have to insist on it. Did you ask my maid to spy on me?

Melania   Yes, I did. The betraying cow.

Elena   That is low, Melania, unsisterly.

Melania   Should I apologise?

Elena   Why so devious when my family have been so entirely hospitable to you?

Melania (*to* **Elena**)   You're a nice woman. Spoilt but nice.

Elena   Wouldn't make much of an epitaph.

Melania   Noble, pure. Look at your hands. Have they ever held anything that disgusts you?

Elena   Disgusts me?

Melania   My life was disgusting. Before coming here, I'd only ever met despicable people.

You've enjoyed a lifetime of protection, adoration.

Elena   Not entirely inaccurate.

Melania   I don't know what it is to be a woman like you, but I do know what it is to drag myself up to standing. I know the pleasure of watching my tormentor curdle and die in his filthy bed.

Elena   You seem, Melania, to revel in your domestic dramas.

Melania   The beauty you speak of – beautiful people sailing off into the sunset – it's whimsical. The beauty I know is shocking, annihilating, it burns through you and its absence turns you to ash.

Elena   You want my husband.

Melania   I love him. I want to cup him in my palm, hold him in my mouth until he hatches, like a catfish.

Protasov   Goodness.

Elena   That would be novel.

Melania   Give him to me.

Elena   My husband is not a toy. He is a man who deals with profound, abstruse, difficult matters of life and death. He's a sensitive man who also happens to //

Melania   Happens to what?

Elena   Venerate me.

Melania   Venerate? Like a saint?

Elena   Yes.

Melania   Lays flowers at your feet? Petitions you?

Elena (*deciding to reveal something to* **Melania**)   Sometimes if I lie utterly still, he looks at me and operates himself.

Protasov   Oh no. Oh no. Not that /

Melania   *Operates* himself?

Elena   Do we have a language barrier, Melania?

Melania   Give him to me!

Elena   I can't give you a human being.

Melania   Give him to me. You don't want him. Give me your husband. I will kiss your feet in gratitude. He can venerate me till the cows come home. I never want another man inside me again.

Elena   You are an appalling woman!

Melania   You ask for honesty? I'll be honest. I have money, you have none. I'll build him a laboratory, a palace! I'll serve him. I won't let even the wind touch him. I'll sit by his door and guard it day and night and I will love him and my soul will breathe.

Elena   Such rapture. You are an unsettling presence, Melania, crudely human. I need a cardigan.

Melania   You can't soil flame with mud, Elena. That much I know. I can give him everything he needs, but he will refuse me unless you let him go.

Protasov   The problem with desire /

Elena   The problem with desire? There is no problem with desire, Pavel. Without desire we may as well be dead.

Protasov   The problem with desire for freedom or // is that things very quickly get out of hand. People keep raising their expectations of life, of what they're entitled to, and we're not there yet. That is what your dream is trying to tell you, Lena. We're not there yet. There is work to do.

Gunfire, nearer this time. **Lisa** *sees that there is blood running from* **Troshin**'s *mouth.* **Lisa** *starts to shake.*

Lisa   And what place in your painting, Elena, will the sans-shoeses occupy?

Elena   They won't be there, Lisa.

Protasov   They are seaweed, barnacles, stuck to the bottom of the ship, dead cells in the organism.

Vagin   Slow the whole enterprise down.

Lisa   Their fate is to perish, Elena?

Elena   They have already perished, Lisa.

Protasov   We all perish, Lisa.

Vagin   Alone in the dark chaos of life.

Protasov   We all perish.

The sound of Lancaster bombers. EXPLOSION. White noise. Bright light obscuring the stage. **Lisa** *is left standing, shaking. As the light dims, she sees* **Roman** *watching her.* **Lisa** *contorts in spasm.*

Act Two

One

Darkness, for as long as the audience can bear it. The black hole that **Roman** *has been digging has overcome the set.*

The sound of a hundred-plus clocks, all set at different times, all chiming at intervals.

Light comes up on **Lisa***, awake, composed. The abstract version of reality that we now see is clearly familiar to her.*

She takes a moment to inspect the hole, then drops something heavy into it.

Chepurnoy (*as* **Gorky**)   Ouch!

Lisa *reaches into the hole and helps to pull out* **Chepurnoy** (*dressed now as* **Gorky**)*, as if pulling a rabbit from a hat.* **Chepurnoy** (**Gorky**) *dusts himself down, looks around, finally makes himself comfortable.* **Lisa***, unsurprised by his presence, observes him.*

Chepurnoy (**Gorky**)   Not everyone saw the island as an Eden.

Lisa   Not everyone's idea of paradise, is it? Sun glinting on the Mediterranean, fishing boats rocking on the gentle swell, the tinny percussion of the masts, the slap of nets on water. The Villa Spinola, pink light slanting through the shutters, the long scented evenings, her fingers caressing a stem. You were happy there, no?

Chepurnoy (**Gorky**)   I was not unhappy.

Lisa   No.

Chepurnoy (**Gorky**)   The food, of course.

Lisa   Of course, the food.

Chepurnoy (**Gorky**)   Stuffed zucchini flowers.

Lisa   Stuffed zucchini flowers. My. My my.

Chepurnoy (Gorky)   My my. Doesn't time fly.

Lisa   So, Alexei Maximovich Peshkov.

Chepurnoy (Gorky)   My name is Maxim Gorky. Nobody calls me Alexei any more.

Lisa   I've been expecting you, Maxim.

Chepurnoy (Gorky)   I suppose a drink would be //?

Lisa   Couple of questions, then I can let you get back.

Chepurnoy (Gorky)   Ask away, but truth isn't truth. To coin a phrase.

Lisa   Whose phrase?

Chepurnoy (Gorky)   The sweaty American with the hair dye running down his temples.

Lisa   Rudy Giuliani!

Chepurnoy (Gorky)   That's the one. The truth isn't truth. And the truth isn't static. Everything evolves. From a given name, to a single cell, to an entire planet, everything progresses. Did you say no to a drink?

Lisa   The truth isn't truth, but the truth is they loved you, Gorky. The Caprese loved you.

Chepurnoy (Gorky)   Overstated.

Lisa   You were a celebrity. Own it. That's what they say now: own it. Truth isn't truth. Own it.

Chepurnoy (Gorky)   Dolce far niente.

Lisa   Sweet doing nothing.

Chepurnoy (Gorky)   Sweet doing nothing. Farcically untrue.

Lisa   I don't mean to be unkind. Nobody remembers everything, do they? We look back, it's all pictures, no sound. It can be hard to remember why we did the things we did.

Chepurnoy (Gorky)   Elena was fond of the fat little ravioli. Filled with caciotta and fresh marjoram.

Lisa   When the Caprese saw Maxim Gorky walking among them on those narrow streets, they peeled their backs from the warm stone and queued up to kiss your hand.

Chepurnoy (Gorky)   I went to Capri for my health. Tuberculosis.

Lisa   Not to mention the exile.

Chepurnoy (Gorky)   Impermanent. I returned.

Lisa   You came back.

Chepurnoy (Gorky)   Not everyone saw the island as an Eden. It was in truth, which is not truth, a melancholic place. You cannot live with such timeless beauty, with that history, without facing the plain facts of your mortality.

Lisa   You return.

Chepurnoy (Gorky)   I return.

Two

Sound of an old radio: 1920s music, intermittently. Ghosts of other sounds in the airwaves, aural chaos (think Beatles' Revolution 9).

Roman *cycles across the stage on a three-wheeled bike.* **Troshin** *crosses* **Lisa***'s line of vision. He raises his hat.*

Troshin   Allow me to introduce myself: Second Lieutenant Yakov Troshin. The same Yakov Troshin whose wife and infant child were killed by the train. I have more children, many children, each one bellicose and empty-bellied, but no more wife.

Lisa *turns to where* **Chepurnoy** (**Gorky**) *was sitting. He has gone. She turns back to* **Troshin**.

Troshin   Wives hereabouts are thin on the ground.

I don't suppose . . .?

No, I don't suppose.

Sans shoeses, madame! Sans shoeses. Fortune is adverse. Very tired, barely standing.

Troshin *begins to shake. He is very cold. His shaking becomes uncontrollable.* **Lisa** *is unable to help him.*

Troshin   Yakov Troshin knows his manners. Simple as that! Yakov Troshin knows his manners, he knows his manners. Yakov Troshin knows his manners. As simple as that, he bids you adieu!

Troshin *exits.*

Italy, 1922. Psychiatric hospital.

An orderly (**Roman**) *cycles back into the scene on the three-wheel bike, dismounts and violently restrains a patient* (**Protasov**) *as he* (**Protasov**) *speaks.*

Elena *observes* **Protasov**, **Lisa** *observes* **Elena**.

Protasov (*evading* **Roman**'s *attempted restraints*)   We are simple folk here. You'll relish your time with us. It's all quite amusing here. Quite amusing. Friends dropping by. Marvellous parties, always so much chat.

And my wife! My wife! A woman of rare discernment. A beauty – quite unwilling, however, to knock up a sandwich.

Time. From a single cell to an entire plant, everything progresses.

Future scientists will look back on our little lives, our small labours, and they will thank us. They will gather our collective knowledge, create a new organism that can think as intelligently as the human mind. And then, then, everything is possible.

Roman *corners* **Protasov.**

Protasov   Wake up, Mother. Wake up, Mother. Wake up, Mother. Wake up.

I write his name in invisible ink.

I open my eyes. He is by my bed, Mother.

Not a stray hair on his magnificent head, Mother.

Fear of death stops humanity from transformation. Hangs over us like a black cloud, covers the earth with shadows, gives birth to phantoms, frightens the mind, forces us to create ugly guesses about the meaning of life.

But if chemistry can create life, why shouldn't it defeat death?

How about it, Mother?

Mother!!!

Elena *assents to* **Protasov** *being restrained.*

Protasov   Life evolves, opens its deep wonderful secrets to the stubborn search of my thoughts. I am the master of so much. I will become the master of everything!

Everything that grows becomes more complicated. Once upon a time, an insignificant, shapeless piece of protein lit up under a ray of sun, multiplied and shaped itself into an eagle, a lion, a man. Time will come when, from all of us, a new and magnificent humanity will emerge. I feel it, I see it, and it is beautiful! This is life. This is its meaning! We are children of the sun, set sail to eternity in a ship of dreams.

Wake up, Mother. Wake up.

Restraints are tightened.

You lied, Mother! Life is full of animals!

Cruelty must be annihilated, hatred defeated.

Why do you talk about the joys of the future, Mother, why? Why you do you lie to me? You've left me very far behind you, Mother. You are the lonely one now, Mother. Can't you understand the horrors of this life, Mother?

You are surrounded by enemies. The animals are everywhere!

Please, do understand me! Do understand!

Protasov *is terrified, his face distorted in fury. His treatment is brutal, ugly.* **Elena** *stares.*

Lisa *turns her attention to the man at an entrance.*

Discotheque, 1977. **Yegor** *is on security.* **Roman** *is smoking. The sound of 70s disco beats can be heard from within.*

Yegor   My wife.

I come home, hands blistered from digging a hole, she's reading a book.

Reading it. A book.

Where did you get a book? I ask her.

Bring 'n' buy, she says. St Mary's.

Hob's stone cold. Feet up. Hole in the foot of her tights. She's rubbing her toe, reading.

I'm standing there. The invisible man.

You're reading a book, I say.

You're some genius, she says, you figure that out all on your own?

Give us the book, I say.

No, she says

No?

I have the book. I'm looking at the book. *Fear of Flying*?

What are you reading that for, you dozy cow? You're not going anywhere.

It's not about a fortnight in Cancun, she says.

Cancun, I think, is nowhere that I'm thinking.

It's a book about perfect sex, she says, where zippers fall away like rose petals and underwear blows off in one breath like dandelion fluff.

Her mouth is moving, words dirtying up the floor.

It's about a zipless fuck, she says, the purest thing, rarer than a unicorn.

And her toe sticking out through her tights, the toe smirking at me. A zipless smirk.

Yegor *dances – it's more like a haka than a ballet.*

The general was a man to command respect. Oh yes. This entire region stood to attention when the general passed by. There'd be none of this carry-on if the general was here. No, sir. You knew where you stood with the general. A man devoid of sympathy. Despiser of the meek. Stickler for rules. Master of obedience.

A man.

A man's man.

A man's man's man.

Not a stray hair on his magnificent head. And his feet, his carved feet. The feet of a saint. And he crushed the roses under his toeses.

His big wooden toes splayed out on the grass and, there by his side, a bud of a boy, a boy sprung from a bud, hurled on to the general's great wooden shadow.

Respect, said the general, wiping spittle from his chin, respect. Your ignorance, your cunning stupidity, no fault of your own, says the general, tucking himself back in. There, there, boy. There, there.

Respect zipless wife. Yes sir.

And her mouth is blooming pink and black, and the general's tongue is as strong as a mollusc.

I will have respect. I will have respect from your rose-coloured mouth, from your dainty black teeth, from your stockinged feet.

Yegor *dances with* **Lisa**.

Music stops. **Yegor** *has gone.*

Workingmen's club, northern England. **Misha** *and* **Roman** *are drinking pints of bitter. On the table is a briefcase full of cash.*

Lisa *takes a seat at another table, opens a diary.* **Roman** *observes her intently.*

Misha *drinks, looks disgusted.*

Misha   As a recent graduate from the institute of commerce, I like to think I understand industry. Daddio and me, we've desired nothing more than to develop local economies, to lend our expertise, our powers of persuasion, where they are most needed, in pursuit of profit. And it's no lie, Roman, to say that I have seen my fair share of shitholes and met my fair share of shit-shovellers on our various entrepreneurial outings – but this, this shithole takes the shithole biscuit.

He looks around.

Corpse of a fucking town. Desolation. Desecration. Kingdom of the fucked. But they all love their football team, eh? Passion. Purpose. Singing in the endless rain.

Daddio's idea to purchase a football club. English, he insisted. Stick a pin in the map. Efficient clean-up of the money, but . . . fuck me. Fuck me.

Lisa *stops reading, watches* **Roman**.

Misha   Sat in the stand with the chairman. Local tycoon. Fedora, mangy-looking car coat. He's in mattresses, upholstery. Young wife in a bad mood, musta got outta the wrong side of the sleigh bed.

Potential, the chairman kept saying. Tradition. Community. Wifey's biting her nails. Her knees are purple, fuckin' goosebumps.

Fuck knows what was in the meat pie. It practically barked.

Fourth tier club? Flirting with relegation? I'd never even heard of it. Roman? What you reckon? Never once been in the top flight, not once in a century.

Chairman, shivering his bollocks off in his rancid coat, has a choking fit when we're talking numbers. Half a million cash? Cannot believe it. Can't process my interest. Fair enoughsky.

Wife wakes up, licks her frozen lips, looks at me like she'd just love to have some extra time with me. And I'm dying of fucking boredom, Roman, my man. Nil-nil after a hundred and fifteen minutes. Baying fans. Penalty. Clumsy fucker puts it on the spot, tries to do some fancy footwork thing on the run-up, slips, hoiks the ball into Row Z. I could have eaten my own spleen with boredom, I *wanted* to eat my own spleen with boredom. The thought of fucking the car-coat's wife in the stinking dressing room makes me want to weep with sadness. It's all so fucking inevitable. It's like it all happened before. What's fucking happening to me, man?

Misha *begins to stumble, then falls, his drink spiked.* **Lisa** *closes her diary, observes the two men.*

Misha   Am I really real? I mean, am I, Roman? Am I real? Because this doesn't feel real. Why did he want to meet us here? Weird place for a handover, no? Roman. The fuck! Roman.

Misha *is on the floor.* **Roman** *stands, picks up briefcase, walks over to* **Lisa***, takes out a wad of cash and leaves it on her table. She smiles, pockets it and follows him.*

Misha   Roman!

Roman!

I want a fucking replay.

Sound of Al Jazeera on the radio bleeds into the Beach Boys (or similar).

California, 1968. Palm trees. **Protasov** *and* **Melania** *are on a beach.* **Lisa** *has a cinecam, recording them.* **Protasov** *is hot, irritated, overdressed and hungry.*

Melania   Save me.

Protasov   You're on dry land, woman. What are you talking about?

Melania   Save me.

Protasov   From what?

Melania   From myself.

Protasov   I don't understand you. I have no interest in understanding you. I am waiting for my lunch.

Melania   I have no peace.

Protasov   I am a great believer in regular mealtimes, Melania, and I have not had my lunch! Years go by, Melania. Years! Lunch! A simple meal. I don't ask for very much. I am a reasonable man.

Melania (*touching* **Protasov**)   In the night, lying next to my butcher, I'd trace a knife point over his flesh, divide him up into cuts: loin, belly, blade.

Protasov   Stop it.

Melania   He slept fearlessly. I have never slept like that. He slept warmed by his stinking breath. The heft of him. Have you ever butchered a hog, Pavel Fyodorovich?

Protasov   I am a man of science, Melania, I have had no call to butcher a hog.

Melania   The first cut takes courage.

Protasov   Stop it, can't you!

Melania (*kneeling*)   Holy man, save me. I'm your slave!

Protasov   Get up, Melania! Get up, woman.

Melania   Give me your hand. Absolve me. Who but you is more pure on this earth?

Protasov   I'm going to fall. Don't. Don't kiss my trousers.

Melania   Cleanse me. Purify me.

She throws herself at **Protasov**'s *feet.*

Protasov   Waiter!

There is no waiter.

Melania   I'm rich. Take everything. I'll build you a tower. Climb to the top, live there. I'll lie down at your door day and night to guard you, protect you. I won't let anyone hurt you. Sell my houses, my lands. Take them, take me. You don't need to talk to me, just look at me sometimes, smile at me occasionally. If you had a dog, you would smile at the dog sometimes, pet it sometimes. Wouldn't you? Wouldn't you? I will be a dog for you.

Protasov   I could not have predicted your desire to be a dog, Melania.

Melania   Not *a* dog. Your dog. Your stupid dog. Your stupid stupid dog.

Protasov   Waiter!!!

Melania   I don't understand your books. You didn't think I read them, did you?

Protasov   Yes. No. I don't know.

Melania   I licked your books. I opened them up and I licked them.

Protasov   I am struggling, Melania. I am struggling. Why lick the books? This is some kind of fetishism, is it? Some bibliophilic disturbance. Hello! Hello!

Melania   You are a man of God. Take me!

Protasov   No, Melania, I am not a man of God. I am a man of science. Stop! Stop breathing on me!

(*Trying to evade her.*) Pay attention to science, Melania, and you will see the eye of god in the mysteries of the structure of matter. Science stares bravely and precisely at the fiery mass of the sun, at the crust of the earth, at the secret structures of stones, at the silent life of a tree. At the invisible particles of your heart. Everywhere it casts its gaze, science discovers harmony.

Harmony!

I am a married man, Melania!

Melania   And when has that ever meant a thing?

Protasov *sits heavily. He is weary.*

Melania   It is profitless to keep two flames burning together. What use can two flames possibly be? You must extinguish one. Blow it out. Blow. It. Out!

Melania *begins to bark. She barks and barks and barks.*

1970s Romania. A street. **Lusha** *is in a trenchcoat, waiting, impatient. Dog barks violently.* **Troshin** *is chased out of the shadows.*

Lusha   You! Show yourself!

Troshin   Pardon me, madame. Sans shoeses. Fortune is adverse, madame!

(*Handing over information on a grubby sheet of paper.*) I am tired, barely standing.

Lusha   Yes, yes, you're tired. We are all tired. Who can afford to sleep?

(*Reading.*) This is it? This is what you bring to me? Kharpov the baker's single again?

Troshin   He is. He is. Wives, hereabouts, are thin on the ground.

Lusha   Certainly at the rate he goes through them. Anything else? Anything at all?

Troshin   The hens have stopped laying.

Lusha *is unimpressed.*

Troshin   Sister Polycarp has a new bicycle.

Lusha *walks away.*

Troshin   Wait! Wait!

Lusha *waits.*

Troshin   The handyman's wife is dead. Holding a book in her broken hand, blood blooming from her twisted mouth. Tooth on the floor that I took as a trinket. The tragedies that befall these restless women. You'd wonder should they leave the house at all.

Lusha   There is very little in this life that is accidental, Yakov Troshin.

Troshin   A wife belongs to her husband, my dear, simple as that! He gave her fair warning. A good long swing of the axe. She provoked him. The family hearth cannot be broken. No, mademoiselle, the family hearth cannot be broken. The beautiful one is destroyed. She let the devil inside her. Simple as that. We crush that which we cannot contain.

Lusha   Fortune is adverse.

Troshin   Fortune is indeed adverse.

Lusha (*beginning to walk away*)   You'll hear from us.

Troshin   Wait! If I could be allowed to work. Collect your eggs maybe. Crawl inside your henhouse, search in the dirt. Hold them in my palms. Carry them to you in my hat.

Lusha   I like my eggs powdered and my informants shod. There is something you can do for me. You notice anything untoward about the vet, you let me know.

Troshin   Untoward?

Lusha   Suspicious.

(*Handing over money.*) Here. There's more where that came from.

Troshin   How much more?

Lusha   Your predecessor got out while the going was good. You may not be so lucky.

Sound of footsteps approaching. **Roman**, *in an oversized coat and a hat, slowly walks past and into next scene.*

Lusha   Be a smart move to get out of this place. Time is slippery, runs out without warning.

She exits.

Troshin   Yakov Troshin bids you adieu. Simple as that. Simple as that.

Roman *hands coat and hat to* **Lisa**, *who searches his pockets as he moves into next scene.*

New York, mid-1980s, art gallery. Basquiat exhibition. **Roman**, *sharply dressed, leans against a wall drinking beer by the neck.* **Vagin** *approaches.*

Vagin   He paints like a leopard. Leaping. Beast of a painter. Beast artist. Wild leoparding beast. Move over, conceptualism. Minimalism? Dead in the water. Give me the fucking antidote. Shoot me up with the antidote, leopard!

Roman *observes him.*

Vagin   I know you? Don't I? I do, don't I? Know you?

Roman *looks away.*

Vagin   Listen, man. In this wild wild nexus of music, fashion, art, to be known is to be unknown. Respect. I get that. The downtown aesthetic has permeated. Oh yes. Yes indeed. I noticed your particular interest in *El Gran Especulato*. Magnificent. Snaffled up by Valentino, I believe. Hard to believe that's all his own hair – placenta pills apparently.

(*Holding out his hand.*) Dmitry. My friends call me Dim.

Roman *ignores proffered hand.*

Vagin   In my role as artistic adviser to the rich and the . . . very rich, I rather famously had a client decorate his entrance hall with rows of individually framed prosthetic eyeballs.

Beat. **Roman** *fails to react.*

Vagin   Eyeballs. He decorated his //

Knew a man castrated a ram with testes the size of cannonballs. I //

Roman *turns to him.* **Vagin** *is a little frightened.*

Vagin   Beauty.

Beauty requires an element of strangeness.

Simple, unintended, unconscious strangeness.

Strangeness is what gives it the right to be called beauty. Reverse the proposition and try to imagine a commonplace beauty.

Roman *yawns.*

Vagin   Read that on a tea towel somewhere.

Roman *finishes his beer, holds on to bottle.*

Vagin   Over here! Somebody bring this man a beer before he //

The eyeballs had impact.

Art should challenge, disturb. To conflate the produce of amateurs, easels festooned with over-ripe fruit bowls, with art is //

Art and sex. Both should make us feel fantastically worse!

Vagin *touches* **Roman** – *it is both sexual and tender.*

Vagin   I know you. I do know you. Don't I?

Momentary pause, then **Roman** *swiftly bottles* **Vagin** *and walks away.* **Vagin** *bleeds copiously.*

Vagin   I know you. I know you. I know you. Wait.

London, 2016. Cardboard city, Waterloo. **Troshin** *begs from* **Roman**, *who swiftly pushes past him.* **Misha**, *in pursuit of* **Roman**, *throws* **Troshin** *some coins.*

Troshin   What a generous world. So full of hope and sometimes offering a small libation! I think you will prevail, my friend. I think that you will claim your right to a future.

Elena *and* **Chepurnoy** *pass each other in the street. They stop and stare at each other.*

Troshin   Yakov Troshin knows his manners. As simple as that! Yakov Troshin bids you adieu!

Lisa *approaches* **Troshin**. **Troshin** *opens his mouth and spits out a prosthetic eyeball, which he turns towards* **Elena** *and* **Chepurnoy**. **Lisa** *follows the eyeball's gaze.* **Lusha** *approaches* **Lisa** *and takes her hand, leading her out of the sequence of scenes.* **Troshin** *packs up his boxes, moves on.*

Three

2024.

Cold, flimsy bedroom. **Elena** *in bed.* **Chepurnoy** *engaged in post-coital inspection of a radiator.*

Elena   Might be a leak under the floor; pressure gauge drops. We're on the maintenance list.

Chepurnoy   Wall's wet.

Elena   Water comes through the light fitting from the shower in the upstairs flat. They're nice people. They bring fresh eggs, five last week. Pavel was thrilled.

Chepurnoy   Eggs, yeah? That's nice.

Elena   They have a contact somewhere. I mean, they don't have chickens on their balcony. I'd have heard them cluck.

Chepurnoy   You have a spanner?

Elena   I have a tweezers. When do you leave?

Chepurnoy   Tomorrow. Listen.

Elena   Gurgling? Gurgling's a good sign.

Chepurnoy   We need to hear a hiss.

Elena   You have tonight then?

Chepurnoy   Yep.

Elena   Pavel will be pleased to see you.

Chepurnoy   You think?

Elena   He talks about the past / all the time

Chepurnoy   Wait! Hear that?

Elena   A hiss?

Chepurnoy   A hiss. Do you want to marry me, Elena?

Elena   I already am married.

Chepurnoy   They asked at the hospital what to do with my wages if I died. I gave them your address.

Elena   Will I be rich?

Chepurnoy   You might be able to afford a plumber.

Elena   How is it there?

Chepurnoy   Alright. I've been portering. After a fashion.

Elena   Growth industry, injury.

Chepurnoy   First few months, the military forbade access to the local graveyard. Shelling continued. People buried their dead in backyards. Summer came. Heat. It became necessary to inter the dead. Medical staffers negotiated; eventually the permission came for cemetery burials to resume.

Elena   And?

Chepurnoy   My job was to carry the bodies from grave to grave.

Pause.

Elena   You look older, Chepurnoy. Oldish.

Chepurnoy   I am older oldish.

Elena   Unless Pavel has cracked the quantum challenge of time, we are both, my love, older oldish.

Chepurnoy   How is he?

Elena   Pavel? He's alright. He got a job! Well, an unpaid job. He's volunteering his services to the Clock Museum. Time, his obsession. There is no agreement on what time is in scientific circles. No evidence to support it apparently.

If they'd asked me, I could have told them it's just an endless sequence of bin days.

Weeks go by and I can't think what I've done. Carried water. Queued outside Lidl. Cooked for Pavel. Fed the cats that gather by my window. Listened to the news. Despaired.

I found eco toothpaste in the middle aisle last week, made of soot 'n' sawdust, and I thought, despite everything, I should think about what I spit down the sink.

Chepurnoy   Lisa once asked me if we loved people out of fear of being alone and I said I thought we loved people despite the fear of never being alone again.

Pause.

I love you, Elena. Always have.

Elena   The egg boys catch raindrops in buckets. I've lost the will.

Elena *gets up, dresses.*

Melania? Do you know what happened to her?

Chepurnoy   Not since, no. Rumoured she joined the Illuminati.

Beat.

One of my jobs at the hospital is to keep their wounded soldiers apart from our own. Their injuries are treated no differently. The physicians say: 'They are patients first, we'll deal with politics later.'

Elena   And what do you say?

Chepurnoy   This war is about who owns the right to a future.

Elena   A future? I'd like to see the evidence to support that.

Chepurnoy   Our future, Elena.

Elena   I spend my life with Pavel, looking after him, bringing him on the bus to his medical appointments. I think about you, about another life I might have lived, of course I do. But this is all there is, Chepurnoy. There is no echo in the cosmos, no other me fighting you and fucking you on some astral plain. There is just this, the here and now.

Chepurnoy   Come with me tonight. Leave.

Elena   My father died last month.

Chepurnoy   Sorry.

Elena   Why?

I was at his bedside, final hours, trying to work out how to get Pavel to a dentist because his breath smelt like incense and he'd been complaining of pain // He's frightened of the lift. Did I tell you that? Pavel is frightened of being trapped in the stinking lift and the stairs exhaust him. Anyway. I was at my father's deathbed, no room for a chair, when he opened his eyes, my father opened his eyes, looked up at me and said, 'Christ, Lena you've let yourself go', clear as a bell, and that was it.

Chepurnoy   He died?

Elena   He died, before I could tell him to go and fuck himself.

She laughs. They are alerted to the sound of a closing door.

Chepurnoy   Pavel?

Elena   We won't do him the discourtesy of lying. It's nothing he doesn't already know.

Enter **Protasov**.

Protasov   Yes. There we are. Yes indeed. There we are.

I've been meaning to look at that radiator. Stone cold. Elena? I am right? Forever stone cold.

Pause.

Looking well, my young friend.

Chepurnoy   Not so young, Pavel.

Protasov   Paying us a visit? Marvellous. One plans to get around to unblocking these things, of course, but my work must take precedence. Elena understands.

(*Becoming breathless.*) The stairs are a challenge. I would take the lift, but Elena worries terribly about the mechanism.

Elena   Let me get you some water.

Protasov   Do you need trousers? I have spares. Elena?

Elena   He has his own trousers, Pavel.

Protasov   Maybe he should put them on then.

Chepurnoy   I came here to ask Elena to leave you.

Protasov   My wife, vet, my wife has always believed that a person surrounded by beauty responds beautifully. There is, as you can see, little of beauty in our current circumstance. In Elena's tenderness, in our care of one another, we have attempted to recreate something of what was lost. We listen but hear no echo of distant selves. Do we, Elena?

So stratospheric is the silence I no longer believe in concurrent selves, out there beyond our vision, making the decisions we failed to make, enjoying the luck that has evaded us. Every unturned corner, every alternative impulse, every abandoned thought, vet, is simply that. There is just the beautiful now to cradle our failures. And yet we have been so lucky. Elena?

Elena   So lucky.

Protasov   I am full of rage, Chepurnoy, so full of rage.

Protasov *becomes unwell.* **Elena** *and* **Chepurnoy** *manage to sit him down.* **Protasov** *grabs* **Chepurnoy**'s *hand.*

Protasov   The egg boys left a carton on the doorstep. For Elena and I to have company, well, what a splendid thing. Eat with us, vet. We can talk about old times. Elena? The vet must stay, yes? We can talk about old times.

Elena *gives* **Chepurnoy** *a costume.*

Four

Chepurnoy *dresses as* **Gorky**. *He leaves and walks out of the dark and into the old set, adorned with plants and trees from the Mediterranean/tropics. Outside, the landscape is as barren and desecrated as an Anselm Kiefer painting. The foliage is fake and the whole place now looks like a garden centre.* **Lisa** *has been waiting for him.* **Chepurnoy** (**Gorky**) *takes his time to turn his attention to* **Lisa**.

Lisa   You came back.

Chepurnoy (**Gorky**)   Not everyone saw the island as an Eden. It was in truth, which is not truth, a melancholic place. You cannot live with such timeless beauty, with that history, without facing the plain facts of your mortality.

Lisa   You return.

Chepurnoy (**Gorky**)   I return.

Lisa   Back in the USSR in '28, chief apologist of Stalinist culture, you go on tour.

Chepurnoy (**Gorky**)   Chief apologist of? //

Lisa   Your ship sails to the Solovetsky Islands in the White Sea, near the Arctic Circle, where the days last for nights.

Chepurnoy (**Gorky**)   You are referring to my visit to the gulag?

Lisa   Was it you who thought of calling forced labour 'humane re-education'? Not as catchy as 'truth is not truth' but close, no?

Chepurnoy (**Gorky**)   You don't understand history.

Lisa   Mate, I don't understand anything. Camp Solovki, hardly Butlin's. A pedal boat in the rain and someone pissing in the indoor swimming pool has nothing on Solovki, has it?

Chepurnoy (**Gorky**)   Make your point.

Lisa   The White Sea Canal constructed by the forced labour of gulag inmates. Scholars and criminals. Twenty-five thousand die. Hunger, disease, random acts of violence. Sentenced without conviction. Men and women. Children?

Chepurnoy (Gorky)   No.

Lisa   Prisoners are fed according to their work output. The weak die, the strong build the industrial infrastructure of the state.

Gorky *reads from his essay in* Sobranie sochineniĭ, Volume 10.

Lisa   Emotional types! Mama mia!

Chepurnoy (Gorky)   Conditions were clean. Husbands and wives were together.

Lisa   For your visit. And the punishment cells?

Chepurnoy (Gorky)   Excellent.

Lisa   Excellent.

Gorky *reads from his essay in* Sobranie sochineniĭ, Volume 10.

Lisa   A drowned ship. Tell me about the boy.

Gorky *reads from his essay in* Sobranie sochineniĭ, Volume 10.

Lisa   The boy. They brought a boy to speak to you. Secret-police officers by your side and you spoke to him for a long time. Can you remember what he told you? They all had so much faith in you, the prisoners. They knew you. Knew you understood suffering. The boy was their emissary.

Chepurnoy (Gorky)   The most beautiful being on earth.

Lisa   You called him fascinating. In your report. A fascinating boy. Did he tell you about the hunger, the disease, the women digging the canal with their bare hands? About the men thrown to their deaths down the long outdoor stairway? Did he tell you about the open mouths in open graves, fed clay?

Chepurnoy (Gorky)   All our histories are savage. Brutal. Do you think we were the only ones?

Lisa   No. Not at all. But I have to ask you, pal, hero, saviour, witness, why did you look away?

Chepurnoy (Gorky)   We could have built an entire aesthetic on beauty.

Lisa   Could you?

I see a man arriving in the penal colony north of the Arctic Circle. It is winter. There is a sign over the gate, blurred by snowfall; it says 'Happiness Is Not Far Away'. There is a window in his cell; from it, he can see mountains and tundra and night and evening and then night again. He will not live long enough to witness the short mosquito-filled summer. 'There are no reindeer,' he writes to his followers, 'but there are huge, fluffy and very beautiful mountain dogs.' The sour promise of happiness that greeted him remained far too far away.

Chepurnoy (Gorky)   What do you want from me?

Lisa   There was a sign over Solovkis gate too, no? It said, 'With an Iron Fist, We Will Lead Humanity to Happiness'.

Chepurnoy (Gorky)   I didn't write that.

Lisa   No. But someone did.

Chepurnoy (Gorky)   The mass executions began the day after I left. The graves had already been dug, the executioners were drunk. One bullet per victim. Many were buried alive, just a thin layer of earth over them. In the morning, the earth on the pit was still moving.

Lisa   I have one more question, Maxim. You stayed for days in the officers' quarters. Days. What did you talk about on those long white Arctic nights? Art? Beauty? Love?

Gorky   We talked about progress.

Lisa   Progress. To what?

The sound of clocks, diminishing gradually to the sound of a single tick. Silence. Blackout.

End.

For a complete listing of
Methuen Drama titles, visit:
www.bloomsbury.com/drama

Follow us on Twitter and keep up to date
with our news and publications
@MethuenDrama